MY SISTER'S A BARISTA

OTHER BOOKS
BY JOHN SIMMONS

We, me, them & it: The power of words in business
(Texere, 2001)

The invisible grail: In search of the true language of brands
(Texere, 2003)

The Economist guide to brands and branding, co-edited
with Rita Clifton (Profile Books/Bloomberg Press 2004)

GREAT BRAND STORIES

MY SISTER'S A BARISTA
HOW THEY MADE STARBUCKS
A HOME FROM HOME

JOHN SIMMONS

To my founding colleagues in 26:
Margaret, Martin, Tim, Tom, Jim, Ben and Simon
www.26.org.uk

Copyright © 2004 John Simmons

First published in Great Britain in 2004 by

Cyan Communications Limited
61 Cooper Close, London SE1 7QU
www.cyanbooks.com

The right of John Simmons to be identified
as the author of this work has been asserted
by him in accordance with the Copyright,
Designs and Patents Act 1988.

A CIP record for this book is available
from the British Library

ISBN 0-9542829-6-5

Printed and bound in Great Britain

CONTENTS

ACKNOWLEDGMENTS

Martin Liu asked me to edit a series to be called *Great brand stories* that he intended to publish as early books from his new publishing venture, Cyan. Having known Martin from his time at Texere, when he had published my book *We, me, them and it*, I was delighted to accept. We then planned the series and agreed that I would write this book on Starbucks. Thank you, Martin: it would not have happened without you.

People at Starbucks have helped me by making themselves available for interview. I thank them for their openness. The further I have gone with this book, the more I have found to admire in Starbucks. Above all, it has great people. I thank especially Howard Schultz, Orin Smith, Soon Beng Yeap, Cathy Heseltine, Wanda Herndon, Cecile Hudon, Thomas Yang, Tom Walters, Kathie Lindemann, Rebecca Burke, Sandra Taylor, Sue Mecklenburg, Dave Pace, Jim Donald, Dub Hay and Marc Stolzman. Extra-special thanks to Carole Pucik, my guide to Starbucks in Seattle and an endlessly patient recipient of requests and questions. The opinions expressed here are mine and not Starbucks'; any errors are mine alone. My thanks and admiration go to the Starbucks Foundation and the National Literacy Trust, which will receive part of the proceeds of this book.

Three books have been especially helpful in my research. Howard Schultz's *Pour your heart into it* (with Dori Jones Yang, Hyperion, New York, 1997) for his personal account of Starbucks' development; Scott Bedbury's *A new brand world* (with Stephen Fenichell, Viking, New York, 2002) for his insights into Starbucks from his time there; and Mark Pendergrast's *Uncommon grounds* (Texere, London, 2001) for its story of coffee over the centuries.

Pom Somkabcharti has seen this book through production with great care and diligence. Rob Andrews at R&D&Co has designed it with real flair and talent. Everyone at Cyan has been a tremendous support.

Finally, thanks to my daughter Jessie, who took many of the photos. And my constant thanks to Linda, who not only read and commented on the text but typed most of it too. I could not have written it without her.

INTRODUCING GREAT BRAND STORIES

Some years ago I was a director of an identity consultancy called Newell and Sorrell. In 1997 we merged with Interbrand, and the merger gave Interbrand the right to be considered the UK's largest brand consultancy. But Interbrand also had a worldwide network of offices in 25 different countries, so "the world's leading brand consultancy" was a justifiable claim.

At that time most of the Newell and Sorrell consultants were deeply suspicious of the word "brand." We preferred "identity." The Interbrand side insisted that "brand" was much more than "identity." This semantic dispute was the biggest cultural problem we had in trying to achieve a smooth merger.

One day, early in the life of the newly merged company, the idea came up that Interbrand should publish an A to Z of branding. John Sorrell and I looked at the draft, and were horrified that A to Z seemed to get stuck on the letter B for brand. Brand awareness, brand dilution, brand equity, brand focus, brand platform, brand positioning, brand relevance, brand resonance, brand strategy, brand synergy . . . you get the idea. Brand brand brand brand brand stretch. The word, particularly when put in such easy combination with another noun to make a phrase intended to convey authority, seemed like the last refuge of a scoundrel.

I tell this story to show how our acceptance of the concept has grown over the last ten years. While just as wary of branding jargon, we are now much more likely to agree that the brand can be, should be, the central organising principle for any product, service, entity or company that wants to grow by creating a bond of loyalty with its audiences. But clearly branding remains an inexact science. We are dealing with emotions rather than hard facts. Branding has, I now believe, incredible power, but its case has not always been advanced by those who have argued its merits in academic texts and business tracts – or, for that matter, in brand consultancies.

This book aims to be neither academic text nor business tract. The same goes for the other books in this series. The first three *Great brand stories* describe Starbucks, Guinness and David Beckham as brands. Contrast is a large part of our intention. One book is about the recent reinvention of a commodity product, coffee, to become an experience that is clearly about much more than just coffee. Another is about a premium beer, nearly 250 years old, that people seem to like for its sense of enigma even if they are not quite sure about its taste. And the third book deals with an English footballer who finds himself playing on a world stage, valued not just for his athletic skills but for his commercial power.

The series title is deliberate. *Great brand stories* sets out to produce books that are readable. Very few business books are. A long-running complaint of mine, while I have worked in the world of branding, has been the neglected role of language. Brands communicate through words, not just through images; indeed, they use all the senses. Brands that connect with audiences through the power of storytelling have a particular magic. That is one of the underlying themes of this series.

John Simmons

A SHORT SHOT

In 1995 I went on a coast-to-coast trip across the US. When we got to San Francisco, the sun was shining and the people were relaxed. We wandered into a Starbucks, the first I'd been in.

We sat enjoying our coffees and the buzz of conversation around us. There's a willingness to share your life with the world that seems particularly characteristic of California. The overheard conversation ran like this.

"I like this place. I come here when I'm stressed out."

"The people seem OK. Not the usual geeks."

"Hey man, my sister's a barista."

Welcome to Starbucks.

Chapter One
Starting with a bean

I was watching **Six feet under**, the HBO series about a weird family of undertakers that has become a personal favourite. Two of the main characters went off to the wilderness with a pair of friends, wanting to get closer to nature. The dialogue went like this:

"Wouldn't it be cool to totally live off the land, to really be part of nature instead of just using it?"

"Not really. I'm going to need my Starbucks today."

You know a brand has really arrived when it sneaks into everyday consciousness like that.

Looking back, it took me by surprise. I think it took us all by surprise. Even though he exudes the easygoing confidence befitting the chairman of the Starbucks Corporation, it took Howard Schultz by surprise too.

Starbucks is a phenomenon. A very successful and surprising one. Perhaps that is why it arouses antagonism and envy among many people, while inspiring affection and loyalty among many more.

I remember my first encounter with Starbucks in San Francisco in the mid 1990s. I overheard the conversation that gave rise to the title of this book, and enjoyed not just the coffee but the experience. I talked with my wife about the lack of a Starbucks back home, and we agreed that it would be bound to succeed in the UK. Of course, a couple of years later it came, everyone saw it, and it conquered.

This was the honeymoon period for the Starbucks brand. It attracted an extraordinary amount of excitement from all directions. In the US, Wall Street and investors bought into it as queues formed outside each new store that opened. In the UK, Starbucks was not the first to enter the market with the idea of coffee plus a lifestyle experience, but those who were first borrowed most of their clothes from Starbucks. Starbucks bought the Seattle Coffee Company and established itself in the UK by rebranding those stores, ready to spread to other parts of the country and the continent. Asia had come a little earlier. After initial trepidation – would Japanese formality allow people to walk out of a shop and sip coffee on the street? – Starbucks basked in the glow of acceptance in Japan and beyond.

Although many could instinctively understand the reasons for Starbucks' success, the sheer scale of it took people by surprise. Sitting in that San Francisco Starbucks I could predict "this will work in England," but even so, the speed with which Starbucks spread was amazing. As I write this now, sitting in a Starbucks in the little English town of Cheltenham, I am aware that there are currently 400 Starbucks stores in the UK. That has happened in less than ten years. No other retail brand has achieved such ubiquity so fast.

Ubiquity. It's a word that is rarely used except, it seems, in the context of Starbucks. A quaintly Latinate word that is spoken almost to put distance between the speaker and the subject. The honeymoon period came to an end around the time of the anti-globalisation protests. It was more a change in the climate than any slowing of Starbucks' development. Naomi Klein's book *No logo* was influential in identifying a number of big American-based brands as villains: Coca-Cola, McDonald's, Nike, Starbucks. The lumping together was a bit indiscriminate, but there was enough semblance of hard evidence to reinforce people's latent prejudices. In a contest between David and Goliath, we all cheer on David. In a remarkably short time Starbucks found itself, much to its own amazement and irritation, bracketed with Goliath when it had always seen itself as David. The general perception was that Starbucks had got too big for our good. To grow that big so fast it must have played unfairly.

We live in societies where we reward and resent success in almost equal measure. We build things up so that they will fall the more spectacularly. Our societies are deeply, and increasingly, competitive. Brands are now an integral part of this. They are one of the ways in which we establish tribal loyalties. Being a sports fan with a lifelong adherence to a football team is one particularly deep-rooted form of competitive brand loyalty. In *Fever pitch*, Nick Hornby wrote about how as a child moving into adolescence, allegiance first to football itself, then to a chosen team, made playground friendships easier to forge. Starbucks provides that kind of playground.

Brands are a shorthand we use to make connections with others and to help define our own identities. The people we choose as friends share similar ideas and attitudes. When we gather it's noticeable how we share similar tastes in clothes, entertainment and possessions. It's true of every generation, not just brand-conscious teenagers. Those most disinclined to agree with this kind of uniformity often have the strongest sense of shared beliefs. So Starbucks gets attacked for destroying cultural diversity on high streets by people who have an extremely narrow range of "acceptable" aesthetics and taste.

The anti-globalisation protestors who were at their most vehement at the start of the new century found a readily available symbol of their discontent. Gathering in Seattle, they found a fast-growing global brand on every neighbourhood street. Ubiquity, ubiquity; they really do seem to be everywhere.

The case against Starbucks was that behind its smiling, laidback New Age exterior was a capitalist predator bent on exploiting those less powerful than itself. The greatest crime was to force a small independent family business out of existence. This probably happened in some places, but certainly not all. The retail technique known as "clustering" – opening up several shops of the same brand in close proximity – meant that Starbucks appeared to saturate certain areas with its presence. These areas were generally where large numbers of office workers were concentrated, the areas where there was greatest potential demand for coffee shops. It seemed surprising that they could all survive, but generally they did. Not only did they survive, but new competitors opened up next door, and many of the independent family businesses hung on too.

What happened was that Starbucks – and it was Starbucks rather than any other brand – grew the overall market for coffee drinking. It seems we now have a taste for coffee that few of us recognised twenty years ago. Far from killing off the competition, Starbucks gave us a wider choice of where to drink a cup of coffee than ever before. As well as choice of outlets, we now have a higher quality of coffee than we used to. For all the cynical sniffing by some, Starbucks is a brand that is committed to offering good coffee. You don't need to be very old to remember the abysmal standard of what passed for coffee in the years before Starbucks entered the scene. The products of Nescafé, Maxwell House, Folger and even Camp did little to educate their customers in the ways of sophisticated coffee drinking.

This then is a story that has unfolded quickly – at least in terms of conventional business development. How did it happen? What have been the ingredients of Starbucks' success? Who have been the people behind it all? What has been the appeal to the growing number of customers?

There is no doubt that Starbucks is a thoroughly modern company. It has grown by instinctively understanding and using the principles of branding. Although it has not neglected the conventional "must dos" of traditional businesses – get the product right, construct an efficient distribution network, earn a profit by keeping costs tight – it has never wavered in the belief that its brand is its most important asset.

The brand itself is built around coffee but, in its essence, it is not really about a product. Far more important to its growth than the particular way of roasting arabica beans is the concept of "the third place." We will explore this further as we go, because it is central to an understanding of Starbucks. But to experience it for yourself, take this book to your nearest Starbucks, sit with the coffee of your choice, start reading, and every so often look up and observe your fellow coffee drinkers. You will see people on their way to work and on their way home from work, students doing homework, business people having informal meetings, friends gathering for a conversation, shoppers taking a break.

I have written this chapter over an afternoon. By choice I decided to write neither at home nor at a place of work. I chose a third place. It was warm and welcoming on a wintry day, relaxing and conducive to writing. No one intruded on my space. I was free to think whatever I liked, to engage with people and my surroundings if I wished, or to shut everything else out if I needed to. The variety of people was a source of interest, yet a sense of communion emerged, a way of being in touch with myself and the world, with my own life and with the life around me.

It all started with a coffee bean, an arabica, not a robusta. From this, as if in Jack's fairy tale, a giant beanstalk has grown that has opened up a different way of life. We should enjoy it, and also understand a little more about how it happened.

Chapter Two
Setting out on the voyage

"Call me Ishmael."

I've always loved the opening line of Herman Melville's **Moby-Dick**. It seems I'm not alone in this. In 1971 three young men decided to set up a business selling high-quality coffee. They agreed on most things, but not on the name for the business.

One of the three wanted to call the business Pequod. Why? Well, he too liked *Moby-Dick*, and *Pequod* was the name of the ship that sought the great white whale across the world's oceans. I'm sure it was the romance of the story that appealed to him.

But his two friends would not countenance the name. They thought the first syllable was particularly unfortunate for a shop selling a drink. They got another friend to do some local history research, and discovered that Starbo was a mining camp from the early days of the Seattle region.

One of them then made a connection back to *Moby-Dick*, remembering that the first mate on the *Pequod* had been called Starbuck. Did he like coffee? Perhaps he did. But the stories of the high seas and the seafaring tradition of the coffee trade seemed to confirm that Starbucks was a name that fitted their business.

The three friends were Jerry Baldwin, Zev Siegl and Gordon Bowker. They had met in the 1960s at the University of San Francisco. San Francisco in the 1960s conjures up images of hippies with flowers in their hair, and that certainly provides the context for the times. Along with the more obvious aspects of the hippie life, such as sex, drugs and psychedelic music, there was a resurgence of interest in alternative ways of life. This interest lasted with a significant number of Americans who turned away from the processed, manufactured and pre-packaged approach to food. They went in search of food that had more flavour because it was fresher and more authentic. They made deliberate choices to reject the mediocre and artificial, and to seek out natural wholesome food. And coffee too.

At the time coffee came in the form of powder or granules, mostly in jars or cans labelled Nescafé or Maxwell House. Its relationship to real coffee was remote. This was true not just for the US but for much of Europe, although when young Americans went travelling they came across a different type of coffee. Few took to Turkish coffee as they embarked on the hippie trail in Istanbul, but Amsterdam, Paris and Milan offered a completely different taste for coffee from the one you could get out of a jar off the supermarket shelf. There was a romance to it as well, because there were trails for coffee drinking that took in the great cities of Europe, and trails for coffee growing and trading that stretched out to mountain slopes and ports in Africa, Asia and South America.

Jerry Baldwin, Zev Siegl and Gordon Bowker did what many educated young men of their generation did in the 1960s. They went away travelling, mostly to Europe. When they came back they settled in the Seattle area, although there was a sense in which they felt unsettled by their travelling. They started working in whatever seemed most convenient at the time. Jerry and Zev became teachers; Gordon was a writer who was starting a creative business. They had become friends because they shared many interests: classical music (Zev's father was concert master for the Seattle Symphony Orchestra), films, literature and fine food and drink. In particular, they shared a love of great tea and coffee and a yearning to find out more about it.

Starbucks started because its three founders cared desperately about good-quality coffee. They had little interest in creating a business empire. Indeed, as Starbucks grew bigger each of them bailed out at different moments, leaving the business to be developed by others. But their legacy was their original commitment to find and sell the kinds of tea and coffee that they enjoyed drinking. Love of the product was what drove them originally, and Starbucks today would argue that the same passion for coffee is still at the heart of the business.

The three founders had a missionary zeal to educate their friends and neighbours in the ways of good coffee drinking. So perhaps it is not surprising that Gordon Bowker's description of his moment of revelation has a biblical feel to it. Gordon would regularly set off on expeditions to hunt down good coffee beans. He had discovered a store called Murchie's in Vancouver, Canada, three hours' drive from Seattle. On a bright sunny day in 1970, his car loaded with bags of coffee beans bought from Murchie's, he saw the light. He later told a Seattle newspaper how he had been "blinded, literally, like Saul of Tarsus, by the sun reflecting off Lake Samish. Right then it hit me: open a coffee store in Seattle!"

Gordon was a writer, so there might be some poetic licence in his story. The hard facts are that he, Jerry and Zev then invested $1,350 each in the idea and borrowed an extra $5,000 from the bank. They committed themselves to the idea that became Starbucks.

In many ways the timing was not great. The first Starbucks shop opened in Seattle in 1971, at the deepest point of a local recession caused by a downturn in fortunes at Boeing.

Between 1969 and 1971, the Boeing workforce plummeted from 100,000 to 38,000, and of course many businesses that depended on Boeing went out of business too. Famously a billboard near the airport said, "Will the last person leaving Seattle turn out the lights?" Seattle might now seem a cool, thriving, sophisticated city. Back then it was a backwater in which the water was draining away.

This did not deter Jerry, Zev and Gordon, although they were cautious in their commitment. None of them gave up their jobs in the early stages. When the first shop opened its doors, only Zev was employed full time. They viewed the enterprise more as a commercial hobby than as a way to make fast money. Above all, they were driven by a need to educate. Bad coffee and tea offended them.

They had a sense of tradition too. Coffee had a history of nurturing debate and thought. They were aware of the way that coffee drinking had become such an intense fashion in the seventeenth and eighteenth centuries. The great cities of the era – Paris, Venice, Vienna, London – spawned coffee houses. People went there not just to take the exotic new drink but to meet other artists, scientists and writers – and to talk. A visitor to Vienna wrote in the early 1700s: "The city of Vienna is filled with coffee houses where novelists or those who busy themselves with newspapers delight to meet."

There were two other aspects of tradition that were important in Starbucks' foundation. The first showed itself when Jerry, Zev and Gordon started looking for premises to begin trading. Pike Place Market has become internationally famous in recent years through the bestselling management book *Fish!*, based on observation of the fish traders who worked there. That book would never have been written, and the fish sellers would have dispersed to other places with less character, if the proposals for wholesale redevelopment of the area in the early 1970s had come to pass. No doubt as a response to the need to attempt regeneration of the city following the Boeing debacle, a group of developers came up with plans for a new commercial centre to replace Pike Place Market. It was to include a hotel, convention centre, parking lot and shops. The people of Seattle voted in a referendum to keep their market and to reject the redevelopment. Jerry, Zev and Gordon acquired a small shop in the market and made plans to open their first Starbucks.

The second aspect of tradition that mattered was the strong sense of connection to Europe. The European coffee house had naturally created its own tradition of coffee making, based on a method of roasting and brewing beans that was completely different from what had become the American way. Like most American cities, Seattle has a link back to Europe that derives from immigration. It has a strong Scandinavian element, and down the west coast are communities that still take pride in their origins in various European countries. Much of this migration took place in past centuries, but some of it has continued into recent times.

One man's emigration from the Netherlands to the west coast of the US is particularly important in the development of Starbucks. Alfred Peet has been described as Starbucks'

Pike Place, Seattle

spiritual grandfather, and there is no doubt that he provided inspirational and practical help to the company. He had arrived in the US in the mid 1950s, settling in the San Francisco area. His father Henry had been a coffee merchant and roaster, and was sadly disappointed by Alfred's decision to follow in his footsteps. Alfred served an apprenticeship in Amsterdam with a coffee importer, then began working in his father's business just before the Second World War. He had a hard time in the war, first making faux coffee from chicory and peas, then serving in a German forced labour camp. But his first and enduring love was coffee and the smell of coffee. It was this aroma that had lured him into the family business and that now, after the end of the war, drew him back despite his father's bullying.

In 1948 Alfred Peet went travelling. He made for Java and Sumatra, and became an advocate for the virtues of arabica beans, fuller-bodied and fuller-flavoured than robusta. As the Dutch East Indies gained independence, Alfred Peet carried on travelling, going to New Zealand and then eventually arriving in the US in 1955. He was not impressed by the coffee he encountered: "I couldn't understand why in the richest country in the world they were drinking such poor-quality coffee." He came to this conclusion not just by drinking coffee, but by working in the coffee business for some of the US's biggest coffee roasting companies.

Everything came to a bitter end when Peet was laid off and found himself unable to find a new job. It was 1965; he was 45 years old and had inherited some money from his father. So he decided to go into the business of roasting and selling his own coffee. He was shrewd in his choice of shop location: the corner of Vine and Walnut Streets in Berkeley, California. For the local academics and students, real coffee, made the European way, had a special allure. Peet's Coffee & Tea opened in 1966, and started selling roasted coffee beans for home consumption. The shop also had six stools for customers to sit and taste the coffee.

For many Americans this was a culture shock. Peet made no concessions to their taste. He roasted his coffee dark and he brewed it strong. Some faces were pulled in disgust, but enough expatriate Europeans sought out the shop to get the business off the ground. Peet was an evangelist for coffee, and he was persuasive in conveying his enthusiasm for the pleasure to be gained from good coffee – his coffee. Soon he hired two female assistants and taught them how to cup and enthuse, and before too long queues were forming out the door. Peet's was the place to go.

Customer service, though, was never Peet's thing. He disliked many of his customers. This was the start of the hippie time and Peet thought many of his young customers paid too little attention to personal hygiene. "Some of those guys were smelly," he said. But despite his hostility and his hectoring approach to coffee education, the business thrived. Indeed, it developed into something of a cult, and coffee worshippers would gather to inhale the aroma of the roast.

Among these customers were Jerry Baldwin and Gordon Bowker. Absorbing Peet's passion for coffee, and dealing with him mainly by mail order, they started to educate themselves about the differences between various kinds of coffee. They absolutely endorsed his preference for arabica over the more generally available robusta beans, and accepted the need for dark roasts. It was like a high-school education in coffee for them. The only way to get a university-level education in coffee was to set up their own business and to start to learn some of the techniques and skills they knew Peet had. There he was, in California's vine-growing area, making his own blends, rolling coffee round his mouth, blind tasting and identifying coffee from all around the world. Could they ever match that kind of expertise? Would there be enough of a market in Seattle for gourmet coffee?

The signs were not good. The local recession was bad enough, but any available research seemed to send out warning signals. Coffee drinking seemed to be clearly in long-term decline. Most companies in the market were competing harder and harder by keeping prices low. Coffee had become the archetypal commodity product.

None of this mattered to Jerry, Zev and Gordon. They were believers. They knew the market outlook was bad, but in their hearts they believed it was because price competition had reduced quality to disastrously low levels. Most of the coffee you could buy was dismal. It was made from cheap beans. It had gone stale on supermarket shelves. Coffee was in a downward spiral created by the big companies who were not giving people the quality of coffee they deserved. Seen in this way, the market actually presented a big opportunity for the kind of business that Starbucks was to be.

ARABICA AND ROBUSTA

Two main varieties of coffee bean are grown today. Both are grown in the tropics because they need warmth and water.

ARABICA

Arabica beans are the traditional coffee beans; indeed, they were the only type available until late in the nineteenth century. Arabica beans grow best on slopes in shade at heights of between 3,000 and 6,000 feet. The higher they grow, the slower their growth and the more flavour they develop. The fuller flavour can be further enhanced by dark roasting. Arabica beans are sold for premium prices because of their relative rarity and higher quality. Starbucks uses only arabica beans to make its coffee.

ROBUSTA

Robusta beans come from a strain of coffee discovered in central Africa just over 100 years ago. Robusta's advantages are its resistance to disease and its ease of growth at levels below 3,000 feet. It can also be grown in full sun. Its disadvantages are a harsh taste and a high level of caffeine. If you roast robusta beans dark, they will burn, so they are roasted lighter and that also has the effect of increasing yields because less of the bean's weight is lost in the process.

Robusta beans cost less to grow and they produce more coffee at growing and roasting stages. As the twentieth century progressed, Robusta became used in blends, then became the basis for instant coffee, and then the dominant coffee variety grown and sold worldwide. After years of being banned from coffee exchanges because of their poor quality, robusta beans are now traded as a commodity product with heavy pressure on prices. Farmers of robusta beans have been receiving less and less money for their product.

With their business philosophy agreed, the founders still needed to settle on how they would trade. The word "brand" would not have been used by them at the time, but they had started to build the basis of a brand. As we saw at the start of this chapter, they now had a name, Starbucks. It was a name with romance and resonance, unlike Baldwin, Siegl and Bowker, which had none unless they wanted to become lawyers. "Starbucks" evoked oceans and foreign lands, and it fitted the sometimes starry-eyed romanticism of their beliefs that their ideas would win in the end.

The name started to suggest visual imagery too. Terry Heckler was Gordon's creative partner, primarily responsible for coming up with the name and now the visual identity. Terry researched marine books in pursuit of a tale that would add another layer of meaning. *Moby-Dick* itself, based on whaling, was too dark and bloody. Another mythological archetype jumped out of the research. Terry found a sixteenth-century Norse woodcut depicting a siren, or two-tailed mermaid. It looked intriguing, crafted, adventurous. Like a siren, it was alluring. Placed in a circle, surrounded by the words "Starbucks Coffee, Tea and Spice," it became the company's logo.

The store itself, near market stalls where fish were being thrown around, continued the nautical theme. It was designed not to look particularly new. A lot of wood was used, and most of the fixtures were built by hand. The coffee was on display: 30 kinds of bean in containers down one side of the shop. The purpose of the shop was clear: to sell whole-bean coffee.

Almost as an afterthought, it seemed, there was space to brew coffee and offer customers samples to taste before they bought bags of beans. These samples were always served in porcelain cups, simply because coffee tastes better out of porcelain. And while customers drank, they could listen to Jerry, Zev or Gordon talking about the coffee. There is no better way to learn than to have to teach, and education was always part of the Starbucks way.

Coffee tastings remain an essential part of working life at Starbucks

Zev was paid to work in the shop through the day: he was the retailer. Jerry carried on working as a teacher by day, learned to do the books by night, and became the real coffee expert. Gordon provided magic, mystery and romance, intuitively knowing that Starbucks was really about much more than an invigorating drink. He and Jerry helped out in the shop at either end of the day. This did not have the appearance of a slick multinational operation in the making.

Alfred Peet was there too, somewhere in the background. Never formally associated with Starbucks, Peet provided spiritual and material aid. To start with, Starbucks ordered its coffee from Peet's and sold it through the Pike Place shop. Perhaps even more valuably, each of the founders spent time at Peet's Berkeley shop, learning the trade and the art. They observed the way he passed on his knowledge and passion to his customers, and they learned how to roast arabica beans to a shade as dark as the jungle. Most of all, he made them realise that there would always be more to learn.

The enthusiasm they brought back with them was needed. There was little time for rest. Early on, the *Seattle Times* ran a glowing review, and customers started flocking to the store. After that, word of mouth took over. Within a year they made two significant decisions to expand the business. First, they bought a used roaster from Holland and installed it in a rundown but affordable building. Once they had worked out how to assemble the machine themselves, they were able to start roasting their own beans. Then in 1972 they opened a second store near the University of Washington. With Peet's in the Bay Area and Starbucks in Seattle there were now two centres for sophisticated coffee drinking.

It is still worth stressing, though, that this was a retail operation, set up to sell whole-bean coffee for customers to grind, brew and drink at home. To help them do that, Starbucks started selling coffee-making equipment, a decision that later led to a connection with the sales team of one of the equipment makers. But apart from the occasional samples for customers to taste, there was not a coffee-drinking experience in the shops themselves.

It worked. The business grew. Quality spoke loudly, and the word spread. The fanatic for quality was Jerry Baldwin, now working full-time in the company. He made the quality of the coffee his obsession, trusting that everything else would follow from that. There were enough people in Seattle who shared this pursuit of purity to make the business profitable from the start. But expansion beyond Seattle was not on the agenda. Starbucks had discovered a niche and would carry on serving it well within the narrow confines that they had set for themselves. A symbol of this was the Full City Roast, a development of Alfred Peet's roasting style using arabica beans darkly roasted. It was a small but significant demonstration that they were their own masters now.

The first ten years were successful but relatively uneventful. Progress was made year on year, and Starbucks entered the 1980s with four stores. Zev Siegl decided in 1980 that he would do other things, and left the business. The day-to-day running of the business was mainly in the hands of Jerry Baldwin.

The original Starbucks store at Pike Place Market

The Starbucks store at Pike Place today – the only store
to keep the original logo

Gordon, having given himself licence to be the "magic man," was rather more dilettante in his involvement. He still divided his time between different activities: he ran an advertising and design firm, a weekly newspaper and, in his vision, a microbrewery. Gordon had ideas; Jerry provided focus. "Quality was the whole point," Jerry said.

It is worth focusing on some of the principles from those first ten years of Starbucks. It will help us to understand what was really solid and what would be taken forward into the company as it developed. The founders handed down their business philosophy, and although they never wrote it down in this form, it went along these lines:

1. **Every company must stand for something.** (*Starbucks stands for high-quality coffee that is dark-roasted.*) That gives you differentiation and authenticity.

2. **Do not just give customers what they ask for, what they think they want.** (*Starbucks has always tried to educate and develop its customers.*) That gives you loyalty and discovery.

3. **Assume that your customers are intelligent and seekers of knowledge.** (*Starbucks educates its customers and selling happens through education.*) That grows your niche into a mass market.

The interpretation in the last sentence of each of these three points is the message that Starbucks later drew from its founders' principles. They have served the brand well, and attest to a consistency that has run through the company from 1971 to the present. There has been no need for massive reinvention.

The original Starbucks was a company "passionately committed to world-class coffee and dedicated to educating its customers, one on one, about what great coffee can be." It had the makings of a great brand, but it might never have grown beyond its product and geographical origins. In 1981 someone entered the scene who loved what he saw in Starbucks so much that he wanted others to share his enthusiasm. Starbucks was not Howard Schultz's child, but he adopted it from a young age and was inordinately proud of it. What he loved especially was the sense of passion, the commitment to quality and the desire to educate people about the virtues of good coffee. The excitement that Howard felt on his first contact with Starbucks was based on his certainty that it would be possible to do so much more.

It might be important too that Howard Schultz was not native to the west coast of the US. He came to Seattle, liked it and stayed, but he never regarded Washington State as the limit of his territory. He knew instinctively that Starbucks would appeal to the world beyond Seattle. He soon reached out to that world.

TELY
ED TO
ASS
ND
D TO
G ITS
RS, ONE
BOUT
AT
AN BE.

Its early commitment to quality and
customer service has served Starbucks well

Chapter 3
Expanding the horizons

There's an American story that I like. It's one of those stories that explode the myth that Americans don't get irony.

After a baseball game, the coach went up to one of the players who had had a bad game. "What is it about you? You've got the makings of a great player. So why don't you perform at that level? Is it ignorance or apathy?"

The player stared back at the coach and replied: "I don't know. And I don't care."

Howard Schultz

Howard Schultz remembers being instantly impressed by Starbucks and its people when he met them in 1981. A few years later, he might have felt more like the baseball coach, wondering whether it was ignorance or apathy that prevented the founders from seeing the scale of the opportunity that he saw. And Jerry Baldwin might be cast as the star player, appearing to shrug his shoulders, pitching for Seattle Apathetic. But we are jumping ahead of ourselves. We need to introduce Howard Schultz properly.

Howard Schultz was born in Brooklyn, New York in 1954. He lived with his mother, father, brother and sister in the Projects: subsidised public housing. His father was a blue-collar worker, a truck driver among whatever other jobs he could find. Life was hard in the Projects, and the need to survive and cope with his environment no doubt helped shape Howard's character.

Howard became the first college graduate in his family. To his parents' amazement and pride, he kept rising, moving from a sales job with Xerox to the head of the US division of Perstorp, a Swedish company that was establishing a housewares subsidiary called Hammarplast. This was 1979, and Howard was 25. He was sent off to Sweden for three months' training. When he came back, his drive and determination made him highly successful, but he was clearly never fired by a passion for the products he was selling. "Who could relate to plastic extruded parts?" he asked in the autobiographical chapter of his book *Pour your heart into it: How Starbucks built a company one cup at a time.*

He was very good at the job, though. Whenever he showed the slightest sign of restlessness, he got promoted. By the age of 27 he was earning a lot of money by any standards, not just by the standards of a boy from the Projects. He married Sheri, a furniture designer with a successful career of her own. To his parents, it was like a dream; he had achieved greater success than they could ever have imagined.

Yet it was not enough. He needed more, but not in material terms. He wanted to do work that would fire his imagination. As a basketball player he had his own hoop dreams: he wanted drama, excitement and passion in his work. And he was prepared to take risks with his life to achieve it.

Because he was good at his job and noticed such things, Howard became intrigued at the relatively high level of sales that Hammarplast was making with a small retailer in Seattle. Starbucks, with only four small stores, was ordering and selling larger quantities of a drip coffeemaker than a mass retailer like Macy's. Why was this? He decided to go and find out.

Until then Howard Schultz had never set foot in Seattle. His job took him across large parts of the country, but this north-western region was not really in the mainstream. The fact that Starbucks was Washington State's largest coffee retailer despite operating just a few stores said a lot in itself. He could justify the visit but at the same time knew that it was unlikely to lead to much. We can talk about luck, but the truth is that Howard Schultz analysed sales information, investigated his marketplace in depth and as a result discovered something interesting to both himself and his company. On one level it was simply good customer relations management. At the same time, none of the big coffee merchants showed anything like this initiative; none of them took the slightest interest in the fact that Starbucks was selling more and more coffee beans. They never asked the question "Why?"

Howard Schultz arrived in Seattle in pursuit of the answer to that question. He was asking it about coffee-making equipment that Hammarplast was supplying. Asked to meet him, Starbucks' retail merchandising manager, Linda Grossman, walked him from his hotel to the Starbucks store in Pike Place Market.

Going there for the first time in 2003, I tried to imagine the impact on Howard Schultz 24 years earlier. Pike Place retains its charm. We have all been to markets, but there is something special about Pike Place. There is still a bustle about the place that comes from the energy of finding, displaying and selling good produce rather than just putting on a show for the tourists. Tourists do flock here, of course, but they buy the marginal goods: the postcards, knick-knacks, souvenir aprons. The business of the market is to sell and they do that with vigour.

Fish sellers at Pike Place Market, Seattle

Fish are sent from one end of the counter to the other, flying between the hands of fishmongers. The meatsellers have caught on and, as it is Thanksgiving week, turkeys go flying. The fruit is colourful and exotic, with pomegranates side by side with all the apple varieties of Washington State. This is a market that looks locally for fresh quality and to all parts of the world for a taste of something different. But this is the edge of the Pacific and out there is the world's biggest ocean, full of fish. It's pleasant to sit at a window looking out at Puget Sound, drinking a cup of coffee, imagining the places beyond.

In American terms this is historic, the peeling paint and the chipped veneer adding to the feeling of authenticity, an age before the big chains took over. Starbucks is the only one of the current big chains allowed anywhere near Pike Place Market. That's because it has been here since 1971, and it certainly was not a big chain then.

Pike Place Market made a big impact on Howard in 1979. He wrote later: "I loved the market at once, and still do. It's so handcrafted, so authentic, so Old World." Here was a man who looked back across the Atlantic for authenticity and, in a sense, approval. This feeling was reinforced by the Starbucks store. If we associate modern America with size, slickness and brashness, Starbucks seemed not particularly interested in the association. A busker outside the door played classical music, violin case open to invite small change. The shop itself was small, but inside it seemed like a temple for the worship of coffee. Like a temple it was filled with a sweet aroma – not of incense, but of coffee. There were dark wooden shelves displaying equipment, including Hammarplast coffeemakers in three different colours. And beans, beans, beans from exotic locations around the world: Sumatra, Kenya, Guatemala, Costa Rica, Ethiopia.

Howard asked the question "Why?" Why did they sell so many of those Hammarplast products? Why did they recommend them? Already he was sensing something of the answer, just by being there, absorbing the atmosphere, enjoying the aroma. "Part of the enjoyment is the ritual," Linda Grossman explained. Howard's understanding of a coffee ritual at this time probably centred around prising the lid off a can of coffee powder, measuring a spoonful into a cup, pouring on boiling water, and stirring in milk and sugar to taste. This was ritual of a different order. The Starbucks staff explained it in the best way they could, by making him a cup of coffee.

The counterman picked up the metal scoop, dug into the Sumatra beans, and poured them into a grinder. Then he put the grounds in a filter in the cone, and poured hot water over them. Meanwhile Linda Grossman explained Starbucks' belief in manual coffee brewing: the need for freshly made coffee rather than the liquid that stood around for hours in a diner's electric coffeemaker. The sense of ritual embodied in the reverent movements of the counterman intrigued Howard. The taste of the coffee at first repelled, then converted him. It was so strong, so different. "I felt as though I had discovered a whole new continent," he wrote afterwards.

Linda Grossman then drove Howard to the roasting plant to meet Jerry and Gordon. Again, the aroma of the roasting coffee. It is true that without a sense of smell we have little sense of taste. Howard was intoxicated by the smell of the coffee, imagining he was tasting the deepest secrets of arabica. He took an instinctive liking to Jerry and Gordon too. He liked them for their absorption in their product, for the feeling he got that they were on a mission to convert people to a love of good coffee. Yet they were very different; they had no cultish uniformity in their approach to life. Jerry was quiet and consciously the good host. Gordon was a maverick with an air of eccentricity, contributing lighter comments from the sidelines.

Whatever it was about them, they won Howard over. For him it was a life-changing meeting. When he got back to his hotel he rang Sheri to tell her he had found God's own country. And Starbucks was the company where he wanted to work because he wanted to learn, to explore, to discover a passion and to share it with others.

As they carried on talking later that evening over dinner, Jerry and Gordon told the story of Starbucks so far. They explained about Alfred Peet, dark roasting, arabica versus robusta beans; the way dark roasting gives fuller flavour but is shunned by the packaged food companies because longer roasting shrinks the beans, reducing the weight of the coffee. There was a clear choice between higher quality and lower cost. Believing in the intelligence of their customers, Starbucks opted for quality.

Jerry demonstrated his point by picking up a bottle of beer: a Guinness. "Comparing the Full City Roast of coffee to your standard cup of canned supermarket coffee is like comparing Guinness to Budweiser. Most Americans drink light beers like Budweiser. But once you learn to love dark, flavorful beers like Guinness, you can never go back to Bud."

Howard Schultz's memory of that day remains vivid. It changed his life, but it also established many of the principles of the business that he was going to grow beyond the imaginings of its founders. Becoming part of Starbucks became an obsession, and when he returned to New York he convinced himself that it was his destiny. But it was not a destiny he could rush into. He had a highly paid job for a big international company. Anyway, why would Starbucks want to take him on?

Howard's way in was friendship with Jerry Baldwin. They met again with their wives in New York. Howard raised the subject of working for Starbucks. Jerry thought about it. He was interested and willing to put it to his partners, but also wary, perhaps because of the clash of cultures between Seattle and New York, between the laid back and the pushing forward. Would this work? There was agonising on both sides. Howard seemed to have most to lose but was the keenest, eager to throw up a comfortable life on the east coast with a big company for the small-company benefit of a decent cup of coffee.

So it took time. A year passed. Several meetings were engineered in Seattle, and mutual trust and understanding developed. Jerry started to float the possibility of expanding beyond Seattle, perhaps to Portland, Oregon, the next state down the coast. But he was fearful of the changes that this would bring with it.

We can imagine the way the conversation was starting to go:

> Baldwin: *"All I wanna do is make and sell coffee in nice shops."*

> Schultz: *"Hire me and you can do that. Give me some room and I'll turn this into something much bigger. It's a jewel you've got here."*

> Baldwin: *"Not sure about that, Howard. But I guess the job's yours anyway."*

That in essence is how it went, except for one last hitch. Invited to Seattle to confirm the deal, Howard had Sheri's backing, his arguments rehearsed, and enthusiasm bubbling out of him. The dinner went well and they all seemed to get on. Perhaps carried away with the vision coming into focus before his eyes, Howard started talking about national and international expansion. When they shook hands at the end of the evening, he was convinced that everything had been settled.

Next day, back in New York, Howard took a call from Jerry. It was not the answer he had expected. Jerry told him that they had decided not to take the risk. He had scared them.

Howard Schultz is not a man to take no for an answer. He thought about things for 24 hours, then called Jerry again, pleading with him to reconsider.

Jerry said he needed time. He would sleep on it.

So he did. And next day he rang to offer Howard the job: head of marketing in charge of the retail stores. For a big salary cut and a small equity share – a stake in Starbucks' future – Howard Schultz was now on board.

So Starbucks had a new marketing manager with a marketing man's instincts. He wanted to expand the business. But Jerry hankered after authenticity, a strengthened link back to his coffee-roasting roots. He could not have been more excited when, in 1984, he got the chance to acquire Peet's Coffee & Tea, the Californian corner shop that started it all. It was like a dream, a hippie ideal come true. But the dream kept him awake at night when it plunged Starbucks deeply into debt and landed him with the problem of commuting between San Francisco and Seattle.

Howard Schultz had other concerns, and the acquisition of Peet's multiplied his frustrations. In 1983 he had gone to Italy to see a trade show on international housewares. The trade show made less impact on him than the visit to Italy itself. He was knocked out by Milan, a city of 1,500 espresso bars where people drank coffee outside the home at least once a day. He was entranced above all by the theatrical, perhaps operatic, nature of the barista's movements. The barista was there behind the counter, ready to serve different kinds of coffee on request. As the barista glided from coaxing out an

The Italian coffee-house experience

intense shot of espresso to whipping up a froth of milk to spoon on top, Howard was already imagining the concept transferred to Seattle and beyond. An instant insight grew into a grand vision. This would work.

"The barista moved so gracefully that it looked as though he were grinding coffee beans, pulling shots of espresso, and steaming milk at the same time, all the while conversing merrily with his customers. It was great theatre. ... It was like an epiphany. It was so immediate and physical that I was shaking."

For Howard Schultz, as for Jerry Baldwin, the coffee was at the heart of things. But for Howard everything else mattered too: the choreography of the baristas, the relationship between the barista and the customer, the warmth, the smell, the sound, the whole experience. Above all, the sense of a community being created, a relaxed and relaxing place for people to gather.

Howard Schultz came back from Milan confessing that he had been overwhelmed by Europe, by its sense of history and its joy for life. He started thinking about how he could bring this coffee-house tradition and experience to the US, but he was keen to Europeanise the American rather than Americanise the European. It never quite works out in equal proportions, but a fusion of cultures was in his mind. This is an unusual starting point for an American-originated brand. In a sense he acquired it from Jerry Baldwin, who was obsessed with coffee quality and learned everything from the Dutchman Alfred Peet. But Howard's obsession was broader.

It encompassed the whole idea of the coffee-shop experience, with its traditional roots back to communities and debates in the Grand Tour cities, and its umbilical cord to Italian espresso bars.

When Howard remembers the trip to Italy, something of the passion of grand opera pours out of him: "Starbucks had missed the point – completely missed it. This is so powerful! I thought. This is the link." The opportunity he saw was to unlock the romance of coffee in American coffee bars: to liberate the idea of high-quality coffee from its location in the home, where Starbucks had always seen it. Experiencing Italian espresso bars had shown him coffee's social power. Starbucks sold produce; it did not sell what Howard believed was the heart and soul of coffee, something that had existed for centuries in Europe. He attached words like "community" and "romance" to his vision of Starbucks' potential as a great experience, not just a retail store.

The owners, though, were not for convincing. The Peet's acquisition was romance enough for Jerry and Gordon. It made them feel that they had come of age as a business, like sons taking over from their father. Alfred Peet had sold his business back in 1979, so they would be buying it from people they had no ties with. They saw it almost as a duty to pay respect to the concept and to the man who had originally inspired them.

This was a crucial time for the future of Starbucks. The owners had taken on a large burden of debt to acquire Peet's. Howard Schultz's strategy – to experiment with the concept of an Italian coffee bar in Seattle – was cheaper. His clash with Jerry was pivotal to the future development of the brand. Perhaps for the first time, there was a feeling that Starbucks did indeed have a brand. Jerry insisted that espresso bars would take Starbucks too far from its origins: "We're coffee roasters, we'll lose our coffee roots." Howard believed that, on the contrary, espresso bars would reconnect the company to its real coffee roots.

Who was right? Bizarrely, perhaps, both were right. The question takes us to the way that the Starbucks brand would position itself. A positioning like "the experience of real coffee" creates a vagueness of meaning that enables both sides to agree while making different interpretations. Brands need clarity of vision. Divergent paths were opening up. For Jerry, coffee drinking remained an experience you could savour only at home. For Howard, the experience had more resonance outside the home; he had learned from Italy that there is a home from home, a "third place" between home and work, where people can enjoy coffee and everything surrounding it: sociability, above all.

Almost as a sop to Howard, Jerry agreed to allow an experiment. When Starbucks opened its sixth store, in the period leading up to the acquisition of Peet's, it was agreed that a small espresso bar would be included. The shop was a 1,500 square foot space on the corner of Fourth and Spring in downtown Seattle, due to open in April 1984. The space for the espresso bar was 300 square foot – half what Howard had hoped for. With no room for seating, it was little more than a counter where people could order and stand. There was a gleaming chrome espresso machine and two enthusiastic baristas who had been trained to make espresso, cappuccino and café latte. The coffee language was unfamiliar to American customers, and so were the drinks.

Howard kept reporting the results to Jerry. On its first day the shop had 400 customers, set against an average of 250 a day in the other Starbucks stores. Within weeks this grew to 800, and the growth was in the espresso bar operation. To Howard, the evidence was irrefutable. To Jerry, it was a source of further discomfort, a distraction from the core business of selling coffee beans, a wrong turning towards the restaurant business.

This might make it sound as if there were constant running arguments, but it was not really like that. Howard retained his respect and liking for Jerry, and he became Starbucks through and through in the way he committed himself to his work. Although he came from outside, he joined for a reason: he loved the passion he saw demonstrated by everyone in the business. He learned at first hand every aspect of the business. He served, he roasted, he tasted. One day he even made a citizen's arrest of a thief, chasing him down the street to recover two stolen coffeemakers. This earned him a round of applause from the customers and did his reputation with the staff no harm.

The more he threw his personal energy into the business, the bigger the gap he saw between where Starbucks was and where it could be. Though he nagged away at Jerry, he was not winning the fundamental argument. Howard saw Starbucks' potential as a brand that delivered an experience that could connect with people's lives at an emotional level. Jerry took a more rational, functional approach, although he was just as emotionally committed. He saw Starbucks' role as to educate.

Coffee can bear a great deal of educational proselytising about its product attributes, but there are limits to the number of people who wish to be educated in this way. What interests us, what really contributes to our education, is what coffee does for us, how it makes us feel. Whether the drink in your cup tastes more or less bitter, more or less creamy, is not so important in the end. It is what the whole experience does to your spirits and your sense of self that really counts. If drinking a cappuccino in a coffee shop makes you feel OK with yourself and at ease with the world, then the chances are you will return to repeat the experience. So the product – the taste, colour, aroma of the coffee – matters, but arguably everything else matters a bit more. This was the possibility that Howard saw, and he realised that it was apostasy in Jerry's eyes.

Plans and visions began forming in Howard's mind, heavily influenced by his visit to Italy. He was considering everything else as well as the coffee: the list ran from music, temperature, lighting, colours, ambience, furniture, decoration and space through to cleanliness. While writing these lines I am sitting in a Starbucks, 2003 version, in Hampstead, London. One of the baristas has just used a hand-held vacuum cleaner to suck up crumbs from the carpet nearby. "Retail is detail" is a popular saying, but it is hard for shopkeepers to live up to it every minute. Of course there will be times when the detail is not 100% right, and in a contemporary Starbucks, maintaining the brand is about maintaining lots and lots of details. Paradoxically, it would have been easier for Starbucks to get all the details right in its early days when it was focused on the product. Achieving the perfect roasted coffee bean in an obsessive way gives you licence to focus less on other details generally covered by the word "service." If Howard Schultz had a serious criticism of Starbucks in 1984, it was that its service was poor, mainly because its certainty about its own product quality led to arrogance and the unintentional belittling of customers whose appreciation of coffee fell short of the Starbucks mark.

The two men reached an impasse. Jerry Baldwin, now owner of Starbucks and Peet's, stayed true to his coffee bean roots. Howard Schultz wanted to see where the thought planted in his mind and heart would take him. He had been backed into a corner where he could either stay, miserably confined, or leave to pursue his dream. He chose the latter, leaving Starbucks to set up his own coffee company. Strangely it was this twist in the story, Howard's decision to leave Starbucks and establish another business, that led to the real development of the Starbucks brand.

He did it by creating a completely new brand. The name for his business was Il Giornale: "the daily" in Italian, the name of a newspaper. Howard's ambition was to create his own version of Italian espresso bars in the US, reinventing a commodity product in the process. As when Starbucks was founded, most of the evidence argued against the new business. Analysts pointed out that coffee was the second most heavily traded commodity after oil. Moreover, it was a commodity in decline, with 20 years of falling coffee consumption in the US.

The arguments simply spurred Howard on. He believed in his concept. He wanted to take something everyday and familiar – coffee – and turn it into something desirable and sought after by building a sense of romance and community around it. His mission was to create mystique and charm, or rather to rediscover qualities that had been lost since the heyday of the European coffee house.

In the second half of 1985, Howard Schultz announced that he was leaving Starbucks to set up a new coffee-bar business. The parting of the ways seems to have been remarkably amicable. Howard carried on using an office at Starbucks while he developed his plans and drew up presentations to raise money from investors. Indeed, one day Jerry Baldwin took Howard aside and offered to invest $150,000 of Starbucks' money in Il Giornale. Jerry saw no conflict because he genuinely believed this was a different business altogether; he still thought Howard was going into the restaurant business while he and Starbucks remained in the coffee-roasting business. Gordon Bowker was also supportive. He provided the name and many of the differentiating principles of the business: he insisted that Il Giornale had to meet people's expectations that it would be better than any other coffee bar.

The search for investors was long and taxing, but need not concern us here. Howard made over 200 presentations, and more than 200 people said no. But enough people said yes to provide the seed money that allowed the first Il Giornale shop to open in Seattle in early 1986. Howard also had a stroke of luck as he started to recruit staff. Dave Olsen, who had run Café Allegro in the university district of Seattle and had become a minor legend in the west coast coffee world, rang Howard up and soon became an important part of his plans. Howard describes him as his coffee conscience. While Howard trudged from meeting to meeting trying to raise money, Dave concentrated on getting all the details of coffee and shop right.

Though Il Giornale started as a single store, it was always intended as a chain. The first outlet became Howard Schultz's testing ground. There he learned how to raise money and to nurture people; to lay the foundations of a brand by establishing a culture and values; to take care of all the retail details; and to see that the fundamental beliefs he formulated drove every decision and set every objective for the business. *Everything matters.* That phrase later became part of Starbucks' philosophy, but it was forged in the gleaming metal and hissing steam of Il Giornale.

Not that Howard sat down and drafted out his values. He simply allowed them to emerge from what was now a powerful combination of himself and Dave Olsen. He later expressed it like this: "If every business has a memory, then Dave Olsen is right at the heart of the memory of Starbucks, where the core purpose and values come together. Just seeing him in the office centres me."

Il Giornale was a brand in the making. It had the obvious outward trappings of a brand, a visual style of its own. Its logo embodied its emphasis on speed: the head of Mercury, the swift-footed messenger of the gods, was surrounded by a green circle bearing the company name. Staff dressed in white shirts and bow ties, and recordings of Italian opera were played throughout the day. On the Italian coffee bar model, there were no seats, just a counter to stand at. Customers could take down a newspaper to read from one of the rods on the wall. The menu was, at least to the eyes of Seattle customers, incredibly foreign, filled with Italian words.

The shop did well, but things had to change. Though the numbers were good, it became clear that they would be better if the bow ties went, the opera was replaced by something lighter, and a few chairs were added. After six months, the store was serving 1,000 customers a day, and a second store opened in Seattle. A third store followed soon after in Vancouver, Canada. Already Il Giornale was an international business, the signal that Howard wanted to send his investors early.

Then in March 1987, something extraordinary happened. Jerry and Gordon put Starbucks up for sale. And Howard bought it.

Chapter Four
Friends and neighbours

Just before I started writing this chapter I travelled to Porto in Portugal. I had been invited by one of the country's leading companies to give a talk. As I was driven into Porto that evening, my first experience of Portugal, I looked out of the taxi window at the buildings and signs that lined the river Douro. It was a pretty sight. Lights glowed, reflected on the still surface of the river.

Lots of the lights were on the tops of the quayside warehouses and they announced SANDEMAN, GRAHAM'S, TAYLOR'S, COCKBURN'S, names that seemed strangely British in this Portuguese setting. But it was a good example of the way brands cluster together as friends and competitors in a neighbourhood.

My fellow speaker at the Porto conference was a French marketing academic called Michel Montebello. His theory talks about the way business and brands have moved from catering for "users" to serving "customers" and now to looking after "friends." Perhaps we were all users in the 1970s. Our expectations were set low. Gradually customer service developed until we all became aware that we were customers. We could make demands, and we did. We chose brands that did not treat us simply as users, but we had relatively shallow loyalties.

The best brands now are striving to gain "friends." Certainly that is what Starbucks would like its customers to feel. Perhaps there is an irony in the association with the US TV programme *Friends*, which often features gatherings in a coffee shop. The advantages of "friends" to a brand are a much higher degree of brand loyalty and a much greater propensity to forgive when things go wrong.

Since 1987 Starbucks has been one of the leading brands moving in this direction. It has simply recognised the importance of sociability to a brand. Howard Schultz might say "Strong brands create a powerful personal connection," but then go on to say "We never set out to build a brand." This is honest, but slightly disingenuous. When he first became involved with Starbucks, he might not have said or thought "We want to build a brand." But because he understood marketing and branding instinctively, everything he did worked towards that goal, including the concentration on the core product, the determination to sell one cup of coffee at a time to individuals. Howard understood that brand-building relies on establishing emotional links – in effect, friendship – with people. You secure this deeper relationship through consistent adherence to a product idea and an experience that goes beyond the basic simplicity of the product itself. He also understood something that certainly was not commonly accepted in the 1980s: that a brand's people are the most important element in delivering a brand experience.

This does not mean ignoring people outside – the customers – to concentrate all attention on the people inside – employees, or partners as Starbucks came to call them. It is simply an acknowledgement that the two depend on each other. You cannot deliver a brand that customers like unless your own people embody your brand. And if there is a lack of connection, the inside and outside worlds both rebel and fail to grant the trust that is essential to the growth of any brand.

These thoughts, benefiting from hindsight, provide the backdrop to the resumption of the narrative. In 1987 Jerry Baldwin and Gordon Bowker decided they had had enough of the business development treadmill. The business they had established in 1971 at the little Pike Place shop was the one that remained closest to their hearts. It was about coffee, pure and simple. Over time much else had been added to it, and these peripheral products and services represented frustrating distractions from the core business of coffee beans. They had bought Peet's to follow their hearts in that direction. Now Jerry wanted to concentrate on Peet's and Gordon wanted to do other things altogether and take some cash out of the business. So a For Sale sign went up on the Seattle stores, the roasting plant and Starbucks' name.

Howard Schultz, owner of the fledgling business called Il Giornale, felt it was his destiny to buy Starbucks. He knew that Jerry and Gordon would sell to him at the right price, but it would still be an audacious move. Starbucks was much bigger than Il Giornale, and as Howard knew well, it had a name and reputation that counted for more than the physical assets of the six stores. He approached all the investors in Il Giornale, and invited them to invest in his bid for Starbucks. He had to face down one of the big investors who tried to hijack the deal, but all the smaller investors remained solidly behind him. He offered them a fair deal, as they acknowledged, and in time they were well rewarded. Howard Schultz acquired Starbucks in August 1987 for $4 million.

After a 20-month gap Howard was back in Starbucks. Now it was his company to run and grow in line with his own vision. But the company had changed a lot in 20 months. When he gathered the staff together to talk to them about his plans for the business, he realised that they were extremely guarded in their welcome to him. People had been starved of information and involvement in the company for the last couple of years as the founders withdrew into their own concerns. Now they were worried about their jobs, their future roles in the business, and they wanted evidence, not ambitious words. Howard was a visionary, a dreamer – "Who wants a dream that's near-fetched?" he asked – but these were people who had not been encouraged to dream for a long while. The "dream big" message was met with some cynicism.

All Howard Schultz had to offer, until his actions and subsequent developments could prove his sincerity, was his passion and belief. He was made uneasily aware that he now stood for the company. His personal beliefs would become the beliefs of the brand. You can choose to believe him or not, but Howard Schultz seems driven by a need to help people make their way, gain respect through work, achieve satisfaction at least and attain their dreams at best. Much of this goes back to his upbringing and his realisation that his own father did not gain respect, satisfaction or dreams through his own working life. In many ways this is an archetypal story of the American dream – the boy from the Projects made good – but it is much more complex than that. At Starbucks, as opposed to, say, McDonalds's or KFC, there is an almost tangible sense that the people and the company's "friends" are united by a common outlook on life: one to do with embracing not resenting the tolerant opportunities of a broader view of life, and with not much room for cynicism. This sometimes exposes Starbucks to attack from more cynical commentators who are not disposed to give a business or a brand the benefit of the doubt.

So Howard knew that he had to move quickly on a number of fronts, addressing the needs of people inside as well as outside the company. His confidence in the product was undiminished, and with Dave Olsen in charge he knew that issues of roasting, making and serving the best cups of coffee were in safe hands. This freed him to think of everything else, to think of the brand, because he now believed that the brand was in everything and everything was in the brand. He expressed it like this: "A company can grow big without losing the passion and personality that built it, but only if it's driven not by profits but by values and by people."

Howard set about creating the basic building blocks of the brand. This meant first defining what kind of business he wanted Starbucks to be, then showing his own people what it might mean to them and involving them in the discussion. Aware that a certain amount of trust had seeped out of employees, he made it his priority to re-establish a climate of trust and confidence, and a sense of fairness and respect. His aim was to create a business that valued and inspired people, and shared rewards as fairly as possible.

The first big decision he had to take had the effect of reassuring Starbucks' people. It also happened to be the right business decision for the long term. The question was this: with the coming together of Il Giornale and Starbucks, what should be the name and logo on the shop fronts? Il Giornale might be Howard's new baby, but he knew that the name Starbucks meant more in Seattle. It had been around for much longer and was easier to pronounce. There was also a feeling that it would be more honest to go with the unmistakably American "Starbucks" rather than the pretend Italian "Il Giornale."

Deciding on a name is, of course, crucial for any brand. Names send signals of intent, personality, identity. We all know from our own experience how names shape our sense of self. Starbucks was chosen because it had equity, but also because it still retained the resonance of legend and mystery that had made it seem such a good name in the first place. Now there was an opportunity to build on the legend.

As always in these situations, the staff of Il Giornale were left wondering. Many of them had grown attached to their Italian name. But they accepted the force of the argument, and the company's new visual identity at least gave them the feeling that something had been salvaged from the business they had been building. Both the Starbucks and Il Giornale logos featured illustrations of mythical figures. With the help of Terry Heckler, Gordon's creative partner and the designer responsible for the original Starbucks identity, the two logos were merged. The new Starbucks siren was less like a book-plate engraving; she had a strong graphic presence that was contemporary, and she was set in a roundel with the brand name in the style and colour from Il Giornale. A similar approach was taken with the look of the stores. They changed from brown to green and were opened out to be lighter and fresher. These were shops where you could enjoy a cup of coffee; they certainly were not restaurants. This

philosophy has remained as the shop design has evolved over the years.

People, as we all know, pose a trickier problem. We all have our own personalities and values, so why would we want to adopt anyone else's? Yet that, effectively, is the pact that a brand makes with its employees. A brand has values; they have to mean something if the brand is not to be completely hollow; and employees have to represent these values. In a sense, this is quite a moral challenge for any employee joining a company that really believes in its brand. Starbucks believes, above all, in respect and dignity to be shown to all employees. If you accept that pact, if you feel able to offer all your fellow employees respect and dignity, that is quite a high standard to set yourself as a person. It is certainly no invitation to join the forces of evil.

Starbucks has been committed to that standard of behaviour since 1987, and talks about its values from the first minute of its training programmes. What emerges is not a cult religion but a philosophy of tolerance. The fear people have and the cynicism they show about brands is that they aim to create a Moonie-like uniformity. What emerges from Starbucks is quite different because an essential element of its values has always been to respect individuality *and* diversity.

But Starbucks needs to do more than just give its employees respect: it needs to demonstrate that respect through its actions. From the early days of his stewardship of the company, Howard Schultz gave his attention to tangible ways that he could reward employees. The seemingly cosmetic change from calling people "employees" to calling them "partners" is one aspect of that.

Two features of its partner contract set Starbucks apart from other companies, particularly those in the food and drink industry. Both date back to the early days after Howard Schultz's acquisition. The first is the provision of healthcare as part of a partner's benefit package. Starbucks has always opted to pay a salary that is better than the industry norm and to offer additional benefits for full-time *and* part-time employees. There is a little bit of altruism in this, but a lot more common sense. Starbucks and its brand depend on the quality of its people. It has always aimed to attract and retain intelligent, enthusiastic, motivated people, but recognises that to do so it needs to offer employment benefits that will feed their intelligence, enthusiasm and motivation. Not only that, but everyone has to be included, because exclusion from benefits will breed resentment and envy.

Howard Schultz was drawing on his family experiences. His father's illness and injury, coupled with his inability to pay for adequate healthcare, had led to hardship and deprivation for the whole family. The decision to give healthcare coverage to partners, including those who worked only 20 hours a week, was made by a sceptical board. But the decision was made effectively by an impassioned Howard Schultz. He argued for the healthcare plan on the grounds that it was simply the right thing to do. All employees needed to be valued. It would build loyalty, reduce turnover, and cut the costs of recruitment and training. Most of all, it would be fair and it would prove that the company really believed in respect and dignity.

This decision made Starbucks something of a rarity in corporate America. Such generosity was not commonplace in the late 1980s. This was the era when Wall Street power players were idolised, when lunch was for wimps and when companies made a point of treating workforces as disposable resources, not valuable assets. But the plan was agreed, and Starbucks became the only US company to offer such benefits to part-time workers.

Since the US had minimal free public health provision, the impact of the scheme was greater than it would have been elsewhere. It was more expensive for the company and more valuable for the partners, so the psychological impact on them was deeper. People outside the company noticed too; a few years later, Howard Schultz was invited to the White House to tell President Clinton all about it.

Some board members had resisted the health scheme, arguing for a profit-sharing scheme instead. Howard Schultz was interested, but knew that, at least for the early years, there would be no profits. The offer would have been a dishonest one, so he decided on a different way of giving partners a stake in the company. The solution he came up with became the second distinctive feature of the Starbucks partner contract.

Howard wanted partners to share in the growth of the company by having stock options, or Bean Stock as it was called. This would make employees genuine partners, with vested interests in the success of the business. Each partner – 700 of them in 1991 when the Bean Stock scheme was initiated – was given stock options worth 12 percent of annual base pay. The following year it went up to 14 percent of salary. Year by year, as Starbucks' stock price has increased, the scheme's value to the individual has grown incrementally. As a result, the company has some wealthy and long-serving partners.

Again there had been questioning of the scheme at board level. Most board members were there because they had invested large amounts of their own money in Starbucks. Naturally they were concerned that their share of the company was shrinking. From one angle shareholders' value was diluted; from a different angle it was expanded. Howard Schultz was an expansionist, arguing that if they had faith in doing what was right for the brand, benefits would accrue in terms of loyalty and trust, leading to growth and profits. For him, people were unarguably the key to the brand's success.

Nothing could have sent stronger signals to the partners. Here was the proof that they were valued highly. Both decisions – to provide healthcare and to offer Bean Stock – were based on the belief that people in the front line have to feel good if they are to represent the brand well. But what then was the brand that they were representing? What was it trying to achieve? What were its beliefs and values? These questions had never been answered in any consistent way or committed to paper. In 1990 Starbucks decided that it needed to do so, and that it needed to involve as many of its people as possible in the process.

STARBUCKS' MISSION STATEMENT

The statement introduced in 1990 reads as follows:

Establish Starbucks as the premier purveyor of the finest coffee in the world while maintaining our uncompromising principles as we grow. The following six guiding principles will help us measure the appropriateness of our decisions:

- Provide a great work environment and treat each other with respect and dignity

- Embrace diversity as an essential component in the way we do business

- Apply the highest standards of excellence to the purchasing, roasting, and fresh delivery of our coffee

- Develop enthusiastically satisfied customers all of the time

- Contribute positively to our communities and our environment

- Recognize that profitability is essential to our future success.

The executive team drafted a mission statement. The idea was to define a set of principles that would then be used to guide every decision taken at Starbucks. The six principles are important in their order, putting people first and profits last, but making clear that all the principles are inter-related. The statement was then incorporated into a deeper strategy planning process that involved more than 50 people in the company and was facilitated by a consulting firm.

What is interesting is that the six principles are altruistic (albeit with an edge), but fairly generic to any business. You could, for example, lift "Develop enthusiastically satisfied customers all of the time" and drop it into the principles of many other brands. It would sit there inoffensively. What gives the Starbucks principles more teeth is that these are meant (and used) to measure whether the right decisions are being taken for the brand.

What perhaps further sets them apart is that behind each principle is an awareness of a particular audience whose needs have to be satisfied. First, Starbucks' own people: the partners who must be treated well because the business and the brand depend on their motivation. Second, the liberal, thinking constituency that Starbucks traces back to European coffee houses. Third, the real coffee lovers, the core loyalists who were behind the original founding and development of the company from 1971. Fourth, there are customers with a range of needs and interests, and Starbucks needs to understand and cater for them while remaining true to itself and its core product. Fifth, there are local and global interest groups, communities touched by Starbucks' presence and activities. And last, there are the financial audiences, the market analysts and investors, but also, importantly, the partners again because they too have a personal stake in the wealth of the company.

Mission statements can be a problem. All companies and brands feel the need to have one. But often they become a dead weight around the business as the mere fact of having agreed a form of words becomes more important than what the words mean. We have all read mission statements that are vacuous because they have been created by people who agree only on the most superficial principles. Starbucks' mission statement still has something of "motherhood and apple pie" about it, yet it is clear that the statement is treated seriously by everyone in the company. Part of this no doubt comes from the decision, taken in that 1990 strategic planning process, to give the mission statement real meaning by setting up a mission review team.

The aim of this team is to encourage comments and questioning by partners in the stores. In effect, partners are asked to question management decisions that they feel are not in line with the principles of the mission statement. Clearly, then, this is not the kind of mission statement that has been produced to hang in a frame behind the reception desk to impress visitors. Indeed, it is a challenge to managers at every level. But if management sets and expects high standards, it has to be seen to live by them. So any partner can comment (anonymously if preferred), and the relevant managers have to respond to their suggestions or criticisms within two weeks. The comments are reviewed by senior directors monthly and aired in quarterly open forums. As a result, communications are open, the mission statement is alive, and many valuable suggestions have been put into practice to improve the business.

All this meant that the soul of the company was healthy. Much had been done to strengthen it: in effect, to lay strong foundations for the development of the brand. In the meantime, there was still a business to run, a business that lived or died by its ability to make and sell one cup of coffee at a time to individual customers. This business was developing into a machine, a fast-running one. It did not deliver profits for at least three years but investors retained their faith and their investment, persuaded that this was all part of the plan.

It was clear, though, that the original management team needed to be strengthened. It lacked the size and experience to deliver the growth that was now planned. Howard Schultz and Dave Olsen, in particular, had established the business on firm ground, but they now needed seasoned professionals. In 1989 and 1990, two people joined at a senior level who were to be crucial to the development of Starbucks. Howard Behar was put in charge of retail operations, and Orin Smith was made chief financial officer. Both men were recruited from outside the world of coffee.

Until 1991, when it entered California, Starbucks had been a regional company almost entirely based in the north-west of America. It was by now a sizeable operation, with 150 stores.

It had a Chicago store that had been one of its most difficult challenges. At this point, a number of fundamental decisions were taken that benefited from a level of investment that was proportionately greater than the size of the company demanded. The investment that was made in Starbucks' systems and organisation seemed lavish at the time, and no doubt accounted for the losses in the first three years of operations, but it made growth much easier in the long term. As the investment started to pay off, new members joined the board bringing with them fresh funds. Most were wealthy individuals from venture capital firms who were attracted by the potential financial reward and by the power they saw in the developing Starbucks brand.

Howard Behar was not a financier. He was a retail manager who had learned how to develop from one outlet to many, mainly in the furniture business. His role was to direct the accelerating growth of Starbucks' shops beyond its Seattle heartland. This meant, at least in his interpretation of the job, working closely with the partners to understand and meet customers' needs. He was quite different from the other Howard. Howard Schultz is a visionary, soon bored with processes and implementation, always looking for the next big idea. Howard Behar is pragmatic and wants to get things done, but that makes him impatient with people and situations that are not working properly. When he joined Starbucks in 1989, the Chicago store was in its third loss-making year. He knew what to do, hiring new staff, sharpening up the systems, adjusting the prices, focusing on the customers.

More than anything else, it was his focus on customer service that made a difference. His arrival in Starbucks marked a virtual cultural revolution. Chairman Mao–like, he challenged everything and everyone, especially Howard Schultz. Confrontation had never been Starbucks' style, but Howard Behar confronted. Obsession with coffee quality had always been endemic to the exclusion of everything else. Why? he asked. What if a customer does not agree with your judgement of what constitutes the best coffee? What if the customer wants coffee with skimmed milk?

As he was to prove, some customers did indeed want coffee with skimmed milk. His philosophy was "Say yes to customers," and he made it a mantra with partners. It has led to the wilder concoctions that customers ask for in a language that is unique to Starbucks: "A double tall skinny hazelnut decaf latte." Whatever; it's the customer's drink. Starbucks will provide the best possible version of that drink. Howard Behar insisted, "We're not filling bellies, we're filling souls." Be less obsessed with absolute product purity if that means a narrow range of customer choice. But be as obsessed as you can be with giving the customer the drink that will meet her desires. Think more about people, less about product.

That was, and still is in many ways, heretical in Starbucks. My first day in Seattle was spent not with managers but with coffee-makers, and they were determined to educate me about coffee through cuppings, blendings, roastings, tastings. The product remains central. Howard Behar ensured, though, that people mattered just as much: both partners and customers.

A DOU
TALL
SKINI
HAZE
DECA
LATT

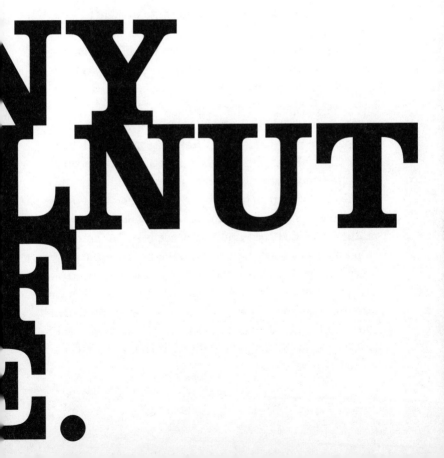

Orin Smith has a different personality and made a different impact. Now chief executive, he was originally brought in to look after the finances. His recruitment was an example of the Starbucks way. Presented with a succession of potential finance officers, Howard Schultz was beginning to despair because none of them "got it." To be part of Starbucks, you need to identify and empathise with its culture. Contrary to the version portrayed by some opponents, this does not mean go for growth at all costs. Orin Smith brought a calm, measured approach to Starbucks at a time when it was becoming frantic. With rapid growth as part of the plan, he brought balance to his judgements, ensuring that a professional approach to systems, finance, logistics and operations kept the business steady.

The danger, and one feared by Howard Schultz, was that discipline might stifle creativity. Yet it soon became clear that Orin Smith's discipline actually freed creative people (Howard Schultz among them) to use their abilities more effectively. Rather than fire-fighting when little things went wrong, the creative people in the company could concentrate on the issues that they could influence best. The front of store could look good and offer a great experience, but only because the back of store was functioning smoothly. Howard Schultz put it in this way: "In business, the front room is what the world sees: in our case, the coffee, the stores, the style, the brand. But the back room is where we win. The efficiency of the back room is really what's made Starbucks a financial success."

By the end of the period leading up to 1992, certain truths about the Starbucks brand were becoming established. They were forced into the open by decisions that had to be made. One of these decisions – a key one for any brand – was about franchising. Given the rate of expansion envisaged, franchising would have been an easy option. Indeed, many competitors went the franchising route and grew faster than Starbucks at this time. Starbucks resisted the attraction of franchising because it could not then ensure the quality of its product and service. Similarly, other decisions were taken: not to flavour coffee beans artificially; not to use chemicals; not to sell beans through supermarkets. The wrong decisions would have led to a loss of product quality that would have undermined the brand. The right decisions were taken: to keep pursuing the perfect cup of coffee, using the best beans and roasting them to the high standards Starbucks had always set.

Of these decisions, the rejection of franchising is perhaps the most significant for the Starbucks brand. It was one of many decisions, as I will explain in later chapters, where Starbucks leaned heavily on its understanding of its brand. With franchising, a business can grow more quickly and economically, but it sacrifices control. While retaining the external appearance of brand control through the application of visual identity, design formats and product sourcing, the company loses influence over the most important aspect of its brand: its people. It is a simple matter of who employs you: Starbucks or the franchisee? Which option will give you a more consistent brand?

Starbucks decided for Starbucks and its own people. It is a distinctive aspect of the brand that it controls just about every interaction with the outside world, as opposed to, say, even a brand like Coca-Cola, which relinquishes its control in the outlets where it is sold. You do not need to go to a Coca-Cola shop to buy Coca-Cola. But you do go to a Starbucks kiosk or store to buy a Starbucks coffee. This is an unusual degree of vertical integration, but it springs from a fear that one bad cup of coffee, one bad experience, can fatally undermine the brand. It calls for an extraordinary attention to quality control at every stage of the process, from growing to sourcing to roasting to brewing to serving.

Franchising was rejected because it would have weakened the Starbucks culture. Recruiting, training, communicating with people remain with Starbucks. But the purity of this approach could not be sustained indefinitely. In airports, for example, there is little option but to work through concessionaires. The first relationship was with Host Marriott in O'Hare airport, Chicago. Airports are natural, essential outlets for a brand like Starbucks: they bring the brand into contact with an international audience that then prepares the ground for international growth. Starbucks decided that it would operate through licensing in airports to achieve its development plans. So there was a retreat from control freakery towards a more balanced view, with the reins kept simultaneously loose and tight.

The scene was set for the next stage. Starbucks was about to embark on a period of accelerated expansion. To do so, it decided it needed to go public: to raise funds through the stock market rather than the provision of private capital. In arriving at that point, though, it had made some solid decisions that consolidated its own understanding of the Starbucks brand. And it had come to realise what it had perhaps always felt: that the brand was its greatest asset. It was the brand that allowed it, almost effortlessly it seemed, to roll out a programme of store openings through the rest of America and, in time, through many other countries in the world.

What were the pillars of this brand? The mission statement and the six principles, certainly. The visual identity, and also the language of coffee that Starbucks was creating. But other things too, that seemed to come in clusters of three. First, the realisation that if you give equal value to your product, your own people and your customers, you will have the foundations of a strong brand. Then, almost mirroring this in its structure, the bringing together of a tight business team, a core of three people with contrasting personalities but shared ambitions: Howard Schultz to supply the vision, Howard Behar to focus on the soul, and Orin Smith to provide the discipline. One final use of three: the all-important notion of the third place. Put all this together, and a world-beating brand was in the making.

Chapter Five
Head for a different place

When I was writing a previous book, **The invisible grail**, I decided to write one chapter while travelling from home to work, day after day, on the London Underground. In my mind I had discovered a version of "the third place." Starbucks has long considered that it provides the third place for its customers, a welcoming, accepting environment between home and work. Perhaps we all need a third place, in whatever form we find it, because it is a space for our minds to feel at ease. For previous generations it might have been the pub or the club; for people today it might be the bar or the gym. Perhaps more by luck than design, Starbucks found itself positioned as the perfect third place for the late twentieth century.

When Howard Schultz began to think about it, he was surprised that the original idea of Italian-style espresso bars had grown into a completely new paradigm. Clearly the idea was now much bigger and more powerful than he had first imagined. A need was being fulfilled, and that need could not be expressed as "for people who love a great cup of coffee." There was a deeper resonance at work here.

A number of people inside and outside Starbucks started to think about this. Ray Oldenburg, a Florida sociologist, wrote an influential book called *The great good place*. He described the need for informal public spaces where people can come together. Perhaps the European coffee houses had played such a role in the past; perhaps American barber shops had performed a similar function. The theory was based on the observation that urban life brings together great masses of people but often leaves individuals feeling isolated in the crowd.

To some extent, all successful brands are social. They bring people together and enable them to identify with others in a crowd without losing their sense of individuality. Some of the most iconic brands capture this duality of individual sociability: Guinness, for example. By drawing on your inner strength, you become all the more individual and true to your own personality while relating more successfully to all the other individuals around you. It is difficult, perhaps impossible, for brands to succeed by appealing purely to the loner. One of the most famous brand failures was a 1950s cigarette launched with heavy advertising and the slogan: "You're never alone with a Strand." People did not want a life where satisfaction was defined as being on your own with only a cigarette for company.

As the Starbucks brand has developed, the notion of the third place has become more entrenched. The music, the seating, the level of ambient noise allow you to feel included in the social place even when you are on your own. One of the conclusions drawn by an advertising agency pitching for Starbucks' business in the early 1990s was that people go to Starbucks for a "social feeling." This was despite the observation that the vast majority of Starbucks customers made no conversation or social interaction in the store. Come in, order, take away or sit down; there is no pressure to be sociable. Indeed, it is this absence of pressure that characterises the third place and makes it a haven for many.

Belltown, Seattle

At the same time, many regard Starbucks as a gathering place where you can either collect your thoughts or meet your friends. If you are meeting friends, the third place takes on a more obviously social meaning. It also provides a setting that has just enough hint of the exotic to be different from home or work (the smell and the sight of coffee beans) and just enough likeness to be familiar (seats and tables that are slightly more or less comfortable than those at your work or home). It provides an environment that is socially "democratic," where the male business executive sits in the same space as the mum taking a break from shopping, or students getting together after classes.

In 1992 Starbucks was realising the travelling power of these ideas. It now knew that its offer worked in north-west America, Chicago and California. If there, why not elsewhere? The only thing that might stop it was a lack of resources to expand and the fear that, if it did not grow soon, the big boys in the coffee world would wake from their slumbers and put an end to the romance. The romance was still an integral part of the company, but there was now a perpetual tension between the functional efficiency required to run the business and the need to keep achieving big dreams that ensured the company had a soul. The decision to go public, to raise funds by floating the company on the New York stock exchange, was taken to meet both needs. Investment would help the business run better and at the same time enable it to achieve its ambitions on a national and international scale. These ambitions were to reinvent the coffee experience in America and to build a worldwide brand.

In many ways the offer that Starbucks put to Wall Street was the opposite of what would normally appeal to the stockbrokers there. Howard Schultz was unwilling to compromise his belief that Starbucks was strong because it was built on deeply felt values. Yet he recognised that Wall Street does not put a value on values. Orin Smith provided a sober, dispassionate counterbalance to Howard's emotional argument. The investment bankers appointed to place the listing did the rest. Even though technology companies were the flavour of the day and even though Starbucks was unknown in New York, the shares finished trading on their first day at $21.50, at least $4.50 above the target price. (The IPO price was $17.00.) The company was now worth $273 million, having been bought for $4 million five years earlier.

The business now had its immediate investment needs sorted out, and a mechanism in place to raise further funds in the future. It could concentrate on meeting its aims, and the expansion plan could proceed at a fast pace. Fifty new stores opened in 1992 and 100 in 1993, including Washington as the first location on the east coast. But competition was growing. The basic components of the Starbucks model were easy to imitate. The espresso business was easy to enter. To open an espresso bar became an attainable dream for many American victims of corporate downsizing.

Starbucks had its Seattle experience to draw on. The phenomenon there had been that Starbucks had grown the market for coffee drinking. The original "mom and pop" cafés continued to thrive. New competitors to Starbucks came in, and the good ones survived. But Starbucks itself seemed to feed off the market conditions it created. Despite constant predictions that the market in individual cities could not sustain so many coffee shops, another Starbucks would open and it would soon fill with people.

The reader can assume that, for the rest of this narrative, new Starbucks shops continued to open. Fewer than 10 shops in 1987 had grown to more than 7,500 in 2003, a phenomenal expansion. The details of that story are not what will concern us for the rest of this book because the pattern had by now been established and would be repeated. The foundations of the brand were strong, enabling growth on solid ground. From here on, we will focus on decisive moments that have tested the brand and demonstrated both its fundamental strength and its ability to keep changing in a positive way.

Growth presents any brand with a challenge to its core products. Are these products inviolable and immutable? Should they adapt over time in response to new trends or developing customer tastes? The traditionalist Starbucks view, inherited from its founding fathers, was that the coffee itself was sacred. There was an Italian way that had become the Starbucks way, and no deviation from it would be countenanced. The debate came to a head over the issue of low-fat milk. The purist view had it that Starbucks' lattes and cappuccinos should be made only with whole-fat milk; the coffee tasted better that way. But many customers disagreed and wanted skimmed milk, whether for taste or health reasons. If denied it, they simply went to a rival coffee shop down the road.

For Howard Schultz and many others, this was a fundamental brand issue. It was for Howard Behar too, but he had a more flexible view and as always championed the customer's cause. As long as the coffee itself remained true to Starbucks' quality standards, customers should be allowed to customise their drinks in whatever way they wanted. So the skinny latte was born, and today it outsells the whole-milk version.

This step ushered in a whole range of product development possibilities. Syrups of different flavours had already been introduced, although a firm decision had been taken never to add artificial flavours to the beans themselves.* But a more significant piece of product development was under development in 1994. As I write these words in the Starbucks store on the corner of 4th and Seneca in Seattle, I suspect that one of the biggest changes over the past ten years has been the nature and size of the menu. It is still not vast compared to, say, the all-encompassing choice of a New York diner where the menu can be the start of further exploration and negotiation, but you can have an extraordinary variety of coffee-based drinks. And Frappuccino now has a panel of the menu board all to itself.

In 1994, presented with the prototype that was to become Frappuccino, Howard Schulz's instinct was to reject it. The idea for the beverage had originated in southern California, no doubt spurred by the temperature. Customers wanted a cold drink. Starbucks offered a cold latte with ice cubes. Nearby coffee shops offered coffee granitas. Dina Campion was the district manager for 10 Starbucks stores around Santa

* In 2003 Starbucks bought Seattle's Best Coffee, a smaller local company that flavours its beans. The SBC shops are not adopting the Starbucks brand and will continue selling flavoured beans.

Monica, and she obtained a blender that she installed in one of her stores. This filled a gap but everyone involved realised the experiment needed development, so it was taken to the R&D department in Seattle.

The department developed a product that used powder, and offered it back to the Californian stores. Rather than smiling and being polite to the management, two other Starbucks partners, Ann Ewing and Greg Rogers, then carried out their own development of the drink. First to go was the powder, replaced by freshly brewed coffee. Variations were made in the other ingredients and the blending process: low-fat milk, more ice, longer blending time. When they tried the result out on customers, it got an enthusiastic response.

Soon the drink was presented to Howard Behar alongside the "official" powder-based version. He had no doubts, and saw that customers preferred the unofficial version too. Additional development and customer research led to further refinements, and Frappuccino was launched in all Starbucks in the summer of 1995. The name was simply a piece of good fortune. The previous year, Starbucks had acquired a Boston company called The Coffee Connection that had an unsuccessful drink called Frappuccino. The combination of *frappé* (from the French, meaning "chilled") with *cappuccino* gave the name all the advantages of being meaningful, understandable and easy to say.

The importance of the Frappuccino story is that it showed Starbucks developing a significant new product for the first time in its history. It developed the product by keeping true to its brand principles. The development process used the creativity and innovation of Starbucks partners, who listened hard to customers. The new product was based on fresh coffee, so Frappuccino was seen as a coffee beverage, not a milk one. And, of course, it was an amazing commercial success, with Starbucks selling $52 million of Frappuccinos in the first full year of operation (7 percent of annual revenues at that time).

There was more to come. Late in 1994, Starbucks and Pepsi formed the North American Coffee Partnership to create new coffee-related products for mass distribution in bottles or cans. The first result of this partnership was a fizzy coffee drink called Mazagran which sounds as if you should be obtaining it on prescription from your pharmacy. Although some people claimed that it tasted really good, sales were slow and the joint venture was wobbling. The in-store success of Frappuccino came to the rescue. It was agreed that, if a version of Frappuccino could be developed that tasted like the store-made version and then sold in a bottle with an acceptable shelf life, Pepsi would put it into production and distribute it nationally. The technical problems were overcome and, launched on a wave of confidence, Frappuccino went on sale in west coast supermarkets in 1996 without any test marketing. In fact, the partnership wildly underestimated the appeal of Frappuccino. It sold so well that they had to withdraw marketing support and then halt production until manufacturing capacity could be increased to meet the level of demand. Starbucks made its then largest investment in a new bottling plant. In summer 1997, Frappuccinos were launched into supermarkets nationwide.

The relationship with Pepsi throws up some interesting questions about the Starbucks brand. Starbucks believes in people and communities, and acts on that belief through volunteering and practical action. The focus of each Starbucks store is local. The company has become big, but remains focused on the small. In many ways Pepsi seems its antithesis: one of those juggernaut American brands that crushes all before it. Howard Schultz insists that experience has proved otherwise. Starbucks has undoubtedly gained an enormous increase in its reach through its partnership with Pepsi, but it has not had to compromise any element of its products or brand. You cannot buy a Pepsi-Cola in Starbucks stores because a big-name brand would detract from the Starbucks brand. The only advantage to Pepsi seems to be the commercial one of being able to turn a profit from bottling and distributing Starbucks' products. On the other hand Starbucks takes decisions that are in its commercial interest, but it will never take a commercial decision (however financially attractive it might seem) if that decision risks undermining the Starbucks brand and culture in any way.

In late 2003, Howard Schultz told me a story from around the time of the Pepsi partnership. The boss of a national cable company met Howard and within minutes of the meeting starting, laid a blank cheque on the table in front of him. "Here you are, fill in whatever figure you want," said the cable man. Howard asked what Starbucks would have to give in return. "Let us install monitors and broadcast TV in the corners of your stores." The cheque remained blank and was pushed back across the table. TVs would destroy the idea of the third place on which the brand was based.

In 1995 the possibility of another joint venture presented itself, and this too was controversial. It called into question the balance between the integrity of the brand and commercial growth. A brand that is to grow, and continue growing, depends absolutely on trust, particularly the trust vested in it by its own people and by customers. The decision to serve Starbucks' coffee on United Airlines' planes threatened to undermine that trust.

The decision came about because United discovered, as every airline must know, that its customers hated its coffee. United wanted to do something about it, so talks started with Starbucks about supplying coffee that would be brewed and dispensed at more than 30,000 feet. The potential advantage to United was clear: its customers would have better coffee and another reason to be loyal to United. The potential advantage to Starbucks was also clear: it would double the number of people it was reaching. But the potential disadvantage to Starbucks was equally clear. If it could not deliver an improvement in the quality of the airline coffee, its brand and reputation would be severely damaged. This was a high-risk strategy, and many people in Starbucks were anxious and uncertain about it.

The figures were certainly tempting. United flew 80 million people a year on 500 planes to all parts of the world.

Up to 40 percent of them asked for coffee. There's an awful lot of coffee in the air, and a lot of awful coffee too. The prospect of reaching and educating an extra 20 million or more people was irresistible, particularly for a company about to embark on a programme of international expansion. The Starbucks brand could travel the world to reach new markets without even opening an overseas store.

If the figures were tempting, the challenges were daunting. Extra new equipment on board seemed unlikely to be acceptable given that airlines try constantly to reduce weight. Water quality would vary according to the country where it was taken on board. Over 22,000 flight attendants would need to be trained as baristas.

At first Starbucks turned down the opportunity because the risks were too high. What use would 20 million captive customers be if their first encounter with Starbucks left the impression that it made terrible coffee? United was upset by the decision, and kept trying to convince Starbucks of its sincerity and willingness to meet the standards needed. Negotiations resumed. United bent over backwards to get Starbucks on board.

Eventually a deal was done that gave Starbucks an unusual degree of quality control over its bigger partner's operation. Equipment would be improved; all flight attendants would be specially trained; a quality-assurance programme covering every aspect of coffee making would be introduced. United was paying for all this, and also for an advertising campaign in major business media to promote the fact that Starbucks' coffee would now be served on United planes. The ad line ran: "After all, we don't just work here. We have to drink the coffee too." For the first time Starbucks had the exposure of national advertising, and it did not have to pay for it.

Everything seemed set fair, but it started badly. There were teething problems with phasing out old stocks of coffee and with the operation of the equipment. The coffee still tasted bad. Starbucks insisted that United had to improve. And within months, United did. After a few months a survey showed that 71 percent of coffee drinkers described the coffee as excellent or good.*

Starbucks had changed in an extraordinary way. It could no longer see itself or be seen as a little regional company. It was a public company performing well on Wall Street; it was in partnership with some of the biggest names in corporate America; it was being talked about in every part of the US even though its actual coverage was patchy. It had also undergone another paradigm shift. In 1984, the first shift had meant that Starbucks offered a coffee experience, not just coffee beans. Now, in the middle 1990s, it had moved its products and brand outside the four walls of its stores into different places where it could reach many more people without needing to increase resources massively.

At this point it was clear that Starbucks had to do two things. First, it needed to take the logical step of international expansion, to step off one of those United planes into a foreign country and test the concept there. Howard Behar was

* Having just flown to Seattle on United, I can say that the partnership is still working and the coffee is good, although it still tastes better on the ground.

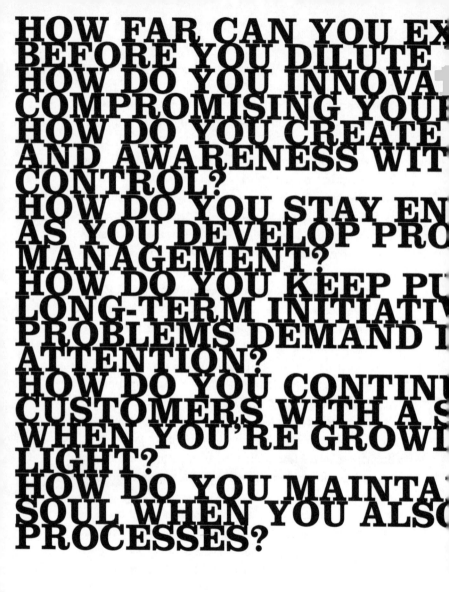

HOW FAR CAN YOU EX
BEFORE YOU DILUTE
HOW DO YOU INNOVA
COMPROMISING YOU
HOW DO YOU CREATE
AND AWARENESS WIT
CONTROL?
HOW DO YOU STAY EN
AS YOU DEVELOP PRO
MANAGEMENT?
HOW DO YOU KEEP PU
LONG-TERM INITIATIV
PROBLEMS DEMAND I
ATTENTION?
HOW DO YOU CONTINU
CUSTOMERS WITH A S
WHEN YOU'RE GROWI
LIGHT?
HOW DO YOU MAINTA
SOUL WHEN YOU ALSO
PROCESSES?

END A BRAND

WITHOUT
LEGACY?
IDESPREAD TRIAL
OUT LOSING

REPRENEURIAL EVEN
ESSIONAL

HING THROUGH ON
S WHEN SHORT-TERM
MEDIATE

TO PROVIDE
NSE OF DISCOVERY
G AT THE SPEED OF

YOUR COMPANY'S
NEED SYSTEMS AND

The problems facing Starbucks as it grew were typical of many businesses.
The questions it asked itself can usefully be asked by other businesses too.

put in charge of international development. Second, Starbucks had to get serious about marketing. Howard Schultz was a marketing man by instinct, and his instinct told him that he needed help to keep Starbucks moving forward in ways that remained true to his understanding of the brand that he had created. He knew that the brand was now out of his control – it was out there being represented by thousands of partners who had bought his vision – but he also knew that nothing was more crucial to the continuing success of the business than continuing belief in the brand. Reinvention was the word he used and still uses to describe the next challenge for Starbucks. In his own words:

"The issues became far more complex. Can a company double and even triple its size but stay true to its values? How far can you extend a brand before you dilute it? How do you innovate without compromising your legacy? How do you create widespread trial and awareness without losing control? How do you stay entrepreneurial even as you develop professional management? How do you keep pushing through on long-term initiatives when short-term problems demand immediate attention? How do you continue to provide customers with a sense of discovery when you're growing at the speed of light? How do you maintain your company's soul when you also need systems and processes?"

These were the questions Starbucks was having to ask itself, and sometimes it struggled with the answers. Howard's concerns could serve as a checklist for any young, dynamic company to use. Any manager of a growing brand needs to find the answers. A marketing director would be best placed to answer them, but Starbucks had no marketing director. Indeed it had done very little marketing in the conventional sense of the word, although it had carried out an enormous amount of brand building. Conventional marketing does not drive Starbucks in the way that it drives, say, Coca-Cola. Starbucks has always operated on minuscule advertising budgets. In advertising terms, if Coca-Cola's budget makes it American through and through, Starbucks' is the spending equivalent of a third-world country. But Starbucks has never needed to advertise heavily. The brand has spread through word of mouth, PR and community activities. Why advertise to lure people to a new store when people are already queueing for a coffee? In 10 years Starbucks spent $10 million on advertising; Coca-Cola spends that in less than a day.

But by 1995 there were some worrying signs. The company had grown at an astronomical rate, but independent research and observations suggested that Starbucks was starting to be seen as corporate and predictable, inaccessible and irrelevant. This was a shock to Howard Schultz, who has a highly personal identification with the Starbucks brand. Because he believes so passionately that Starbucks is based on individuality and diversity, and on its ability to create communities, any criticism of Starbucks becomes a personal slight. The research findings reinforced the need to have a senior marketing executive on board.

Scott Bedbury was identified as the person for the job. Having made his name at Nike, he came to Starbucks after a lot of persuasion from Howard Schultz. He had helped Nike grow through a clear concentration on what the brand was really about, combined with innovative marketing campaigns and hefty advertising programmes. From his time there (1987–94) came the internal brand mantra "Authentic athletic performance" to act as a touchstone for judging activities as true or false to the brand. The external expression of this single-mindedness was the line "Just do it'" which has since become inseparable from Nike. It serves as a good example of the need for brands to be consistent and committed to their core ideas. The truth is, more or less any company in the 1980s could have come up with "Just do it" and fitted it to their brand. But only Nike did it and kept just doing it; and, as in sport, the more they practised, the luckier they got.

Scott Bedbury left Nike in 1994 with the intention of writing a book about brands based on his own experiences. He was using a log cabin as a writer's retreat when Howard Schultz rang him. He was invited to Seattle and eventually agreed to become chief marketing executive for Starbucks at the beginning of 1995. He stayed for three years before independent consultancy and that shelved project to write a book lured him away again. But in that time he helped Starbucks to raise its game to a new level.

Scott found Starbucks a completely different animal from Nike. He was given a marketing budget of just $5 million, the sort of figure that would see Nike through a few days of advertising in a quiet period. So he needed to husband his resources and spend his money wisely.

The first thing he needed was more information, so he embarked on a process he called The Big Dig. He recruited an ex-colleague, Jerome Conlon, who had been Nike's head of consumer insights. For the next nine months they carried out – in a very hands-on way because there was no budget – a comprehensive research study into the way customers and potential customers regarded Starbucks. They discovered many things, some worrying, some reassuring, and started to get a feel for who made up the Starbucks audience. It seemed that Starbucks was meeting the needs of 30- and 40-year-olds, but not really reaching out to younger groups, in particular college students. Above all, it was not getting its story across well: people became interested or even converted once they heard more.

The most important insight from the research was that coffee is always much more than just a drink. It's surrounded by emotion. It comes with an experience and an expectation of its own: partly to do with the kind of coffee house where you now expect to drink it, partly to do with the long tradition of European coffee houses.

The conclusion reached was that the core of the Starbucks brand was less about making a great cup of coffee than with providing a great experience accompanied by coffee. This was a conclusion that the original founders of Starbucks might have felt uncomfortable with. For them it was all about supplying a product and educating customers in the ways of choosing and making the best coffee. The message for Starbucks in 1995 was different. Of course, the coffee itself still mattered: the fact that the beans were carefully grown, selected, roasted, brewed with good water and not allowed to stew in the style of the traditional US diner. But all this seemed pretty obvious to customers: Starbucks sells coffee. We know it's good coffee. What about everything else? This is in no way to deny the importance of the product. Getting the coffee right is the basis of establishing trust, which then gives your brand permission to connect people to other possibilities and establish deeper relationships. But the product is not the brand; it is simply an important part of the brand experience.

Scott Bedbury was able to use the knowledge gained from The Big Dig to add richness and clarity to the Starbucks brand. The research supported the brand's values but suggested that Starbucks was not being particularly effective in communicating them. Starbucks should be able to develop a style of advertising, even if not a scale of advertising, that would attract more notice and affection. The Big Dig also provided a foundation of information on which Starbucks could now start to design the store of the future. The architectural and design team played creatively with the possibilities, coming up with colour palettes, stories about the sea and myths about sirens, illustrations and photographs, textures and textiles, furniture and accessories. As they did so they started to create mood boards, sticking fragments of words and images down until they evolved into the mural styles that are still current in Starbucks stores today.

The design exploration was given guidance and parameters. First, to delve deep into the brand, building on knowledge from The Big Dig. Second, to learn from fast-food outlets but to discard most of that learning, keeping only what would sit with Starbucks values. Third, to create a more expansive palette of colours and imagery. Finally, as if in total contradiction, to reduce costs by 25 percent. Tough and contradictory as it looked, the brief hung together with the findings from research: that, for example, students wanted Starbucks to be funkier, a freer spirit, a place where they could hang out without feeling the pressure of a fast-food outlet's speed, high-tech efficiency and glaring lighting. They wanted a place for people, not a place to be processed as a customer unit.

The question being asked was challenging. How do you open 300 stores a year, each one of them distinctive and designed to fit the tone of the local neighbourhood? It was a heartfelt and increasingly urgent question as the pace of store openings quickened and international openings added a further complication to the mix. Store design changed more radically than might have been expected, given the pressures on time and cost. Rather than moving towards greater uniformity – neat solutions that could be packaged and rolled out – design generated a new sense of creativity and adventure, influenced by and influencing the kinds of space being acquired. There was movement towards grand cafés, flagship stores with fireplaces and architectural features, mixing high ceilings with comfortable alcoves. Into these spaces were introduced leather chairs, fabric-covered sofas, newspapers and an attitude of non-conformity.

Structure and discipline were needed, however. These were provided by the brand itself. Difficult decisions were referred

Starbucks stores in Ginza *(top)*, Shanghai *(middle)* and Switzerland *(bottom)*

to the brand's principles and values. For example, what kind of cups should coffee be served from? Though polystyrene was much cheaper, recyclable paper cups with a paper sleeve were chosen; they looked nicer and were better for the environment. Customers drinking coffee in the store would still be given porcelain cups because they added pleasure to the experience. Other companies would take different decisions – to cut costs, to ignore the environmental impact – but that way you end up in a business without soul and one that is not really sustainable in the long term. The expedient decisions you make undermine all sense of differentiation and personality, and give people little reason to like you and stay loyal. A brand is a hard taskmaster, forcing companies to live up to their principles or forfeit the trust on which they depend.

Graphic design imposed its own disciplines that also derived from the brand. Grasping the need to embrace diversity and respect individuality, the Starbucks design team rejected the sterile option of a single look for all the stores. They explored and developed variations drawing on the four elements of earth, fire, water and air, which were then related to four stages of coffee-making: grow, roast, brew and aroma. This provides an intellectual and aesthetic elegance, but is it too neat? Why is "aroma" a stage of coffee making rather than, say, "serve"? The answer is that Starbucks is interested in the senses so that it can create a true coffee experience. Aroma is integral to the coffee itself.

Does it work in practice? It does, because it provides a rich matrix of possibilities, all anchored to core ideas in the

Starbucks brand. For example, the colour palettes offer consistency within variety. The "grow" design scheme is predominantly green. "Roast" is shades of red and brown. "Brew" brings in more blue for water. And "aroma" is lighter pastels, with yellows, greens and whites. But the idea is for each scheme to work harmoniously with the others, so in many ways the quintessential Starbucks design is for a shop that is spacious and separated into different compartments, rich in the diversity of the design but deep in its sources. Other design disciplines follow this lead. Different materials can be specified for furniture within each of the themes, but these are not a set list. You can vary them, adding or discarding elements to make a store idiosyncratic.

Even within Seattle the contrast the design achieves while maintaining a clear Starbucks feel is impressive. The store on 23rd and Jackson, in a predominantly African-American area famous for its jazz history, has a community-painted mural on one wall with black and white photographs from the 1940s all around. The photos – stylish shots by Al Smith of Quincy Jones, Ray Charles and other jazz greats who played in the area – provide a backdrop for new musical activity from the students of the neighbouring arts college.

Just a few miles down the road, the neighbourhood of Belltown is completely different, and so is the store. Belltown is like New York's SoHo: bohemian, arty and laid back. The Art Institute of Seattle is nearby and its students hang their works on one wall of the store, creating exhibitions that change every two months. If paintings are sold, the money

goes direct to the student artists. The collegiate, artistic feel continues with the furniture, old if not antique, with another wall featuring individual mirrors in ornate frames. The whole is designed like the extension of a living room inhabited by Armistead Maupin's Mrs Madrigal.

In between these shops are scores of others, all individual and different, yet all unmistakably Starbucks. It's a difficult trick for any brand to pull off, but Starbucks does it not just across one American city but every US state and 32 different countries.

The foundations were made strong by the work of Scott Bedbury. The greatest advantage from the kind of information followed by analysis that Scott instituted was that from 1996 onwards, and perhaps for the first time, Starbucks had a rational means of making decisions about how to develop its business. The brand provided a touchstone, a steady guide to decision making. Previously Starbucks had relied simply on the intuition of Howard Schultz and its own people. Those who "got" the brand but could not articulate it, and those who did not "get" the brand and so could not fully accept its obligations, were sometimes left agonising. As Starbucks got bigger, the danger that people would not have that intuitive understanding grew. The wrong decisions could easily be made for perfectly good reasons. For example, opportunities kept coming up to sell more volume through a partnership, and to make more money as a result. Now, with a stronger sense of what the brand stood for, it was easier to say no to ventures that might make money in the short term but destroy reputation in the longer term.

A tool that Scott Bedbury imported from Nike was the brand mantra. This is simply a short phrase – not a strapline that runs in advertising – that sets out the essence of the brand. It is not something that the outside world ever sees or hears through direct communication. Indeed, many of the internal audience may never hear the mantra presented, although they should all be able to recognise its truth. But the philosophy behind it is never frame it, never put it on the wall.

For Starbucks the equivalent of Nike's "Authentic athletic performance" became "Rewarding everyday moments." No mention of coffee, although the mantra clearly fits with the idea of treating yourself to a coffee, a Frappuccino, a tea, a juice, a muffin, a quiet read or an animated conversation. As a description, it is tight enough to the brand but also baggy enough to allow creative development over time. The mantra works because it taps into the emotional triggers of the brand, the need to reward ourselves in stressful times, to rise above the humdrum, to see the possibility of the extraordinary in the ordinary. When we drink a cup of coffee in Starbucks we are fulfilling a deeper need than the quenching of thirst. As Scott Bedbury put it: "Consciously or not, we seek experiences that make us think, that make us feel, that help us grow, and that enrich our lives in some way."

The longevity of this approach was brought home to me in October 2003, eight years after The Big Dig. I visited the newly refurbished Hayward Gallery on London's South Bank to see an art exhibition. Afterwards I went into the new Starbucks located inside the gallery. It's an elegant little shop, with stylish furniture that sits with the feel of an art gallery, providing "the finest coffee and stimulating art in a space where you can be inspired, connect, escape and enjoy." And on the chalk board, the following words have been handwritten by the barista: "Starbucks at the Hayward. Art demands time and thought. Good excuse for a muffin."

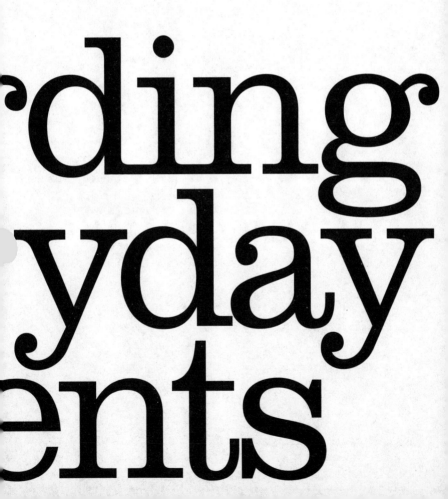

Chapter Six
Here, there and everywhere

You know when a brand has become an everyday part of our lives. It enters popular consciousness and becomes a reference point that everyone understands and laughs at. In the 1990s the comedian Janeane Garofalo appeared on a TV comedy show and joked "They just opened a Starbucks – in my living room."

Equally you know that a brand has reached a position of confidence about itself when it uses such jokes in its annual general meeting. Investors at the introduction of the 2003 annual report were shown a video with a whole succession of clips about Starbucks, including the following from a spoof news report: "The iceberg is easy to spot because it's 50 miles long and has three Starbucks."

From this it seems that Starbucks has come to terms with its own ubiquity. Perhaps it senses that the world has too. Over the last ten years, life for Starbucks has been a roller-coaster ride, but two particular streams have consistently run through everything. The first is increasing internationalisation, which will be dealt with in this chapter. The second, against the background of debates about globalisation and a growing distrust of corporate America, is Starbucks' commitment to communities, which I will cover in the next chapter.

By 1995 Starbucks had emerged as the US speciality roaster that could bring you real coffee in the form of beans to your home or an espresso to your high street. The big coffee merchants had overslept; they simply had not noticed the significance of what was happening. Yet Starbucks was still a North American phenomenon. The company had expanded out of its north-western corner of the US into the major cities and into parts of Canada. It had even opened in New York, despite misgivings and analysts' doubts about whether the concept was truly portable. Queues outside the shop seemed to indicate that it was. In many ways New York strikes me as a separate country within America. Perhaps "conquering" it gave Starbucks the final proof it needed that it could and should export its concept to other countries. To do so, it put Howard Behar in charge of international development.

It was a sign of growing confidence in the brand. Starbucks had always insisted on the need to build the brand one cup at a time, one person at a time, and this focus on the individual customer became one of the building blocks of the brand.

Indeed, "one brick at a time" seemed to be the way the brand was built strong. The third place. The mission statement. The principles and values. The brand mantra. There were now many building blocks that reinforced each other, whereas with other brands such a plethora of statements would imply internal contradictions and confusion.

One other statement of positioning, associated with the concept of the third place, became another of these building blocks. The statement went along these lines: Starbucks offers a *taste of romance* because it provides a touch of the exotic in everyday life, with coffees from around the world. It is an *affordable luxury* that brings a certain democracy because its products, although often premium priced, are still reasonable as a treat to most people. Starbucks provides an *oasis* where people can take quiet moments to gather themselves and their thoughts. And it offers a place for *casual social interaction* that works even though the result is often the sociability of being out in the world while remaining private with your own thoughts.

In even simpler terms, it became clear that for customers, the Starbucks brand was in almost equal parts about the *coffee*, the *people* and the *experience*. The way this was achieved was through a word that is one of Howard Schultz's favourites: romance. So Starbucks needs to *romance the bean*, which means being fanatical about the quality of the coffee bean itself and about every step that is taken to place a cup of coffee before the customer. It means sourcing the best arabica beans, shipping and storing well, roasting the beans to an

The range of Starbucks' coffee is part of the romance of the bean

PERU
STARBUCKS COFFEE
BALANCED & ROUND
MILD

PUERTO RICO
STARBUCKS COFFEE
DELICATE & SOFT
MILD

ARABIAN MOCHA SANANI
starbucks coffee
WILD & EXOTIC
BOLD

starbucks coffee
Serena Organic Blend™
LIVELY & COMPLEX
SMOOTH

ETHIOPIA SIDAMO
THE BIRTHPLACE OF COFFEE
ISSUED
STARBUCKS COFFEE
LEMONY WITH FLORAL AROMA
BOLD

STARBUCKS®
SPECIAL RESERVE
Harvest 2003
A complex flavor balanced with cocoa and winey notes.
2003 BLEND

starbucks coffee
Sulawesi
SMOOTH & ELEGANT
BOLD

SUMATRA
STARBUCKS COFFEE
EARTHY & AROMATIC
BOLD

STARBUCKS COFFEE
Tanzania
CITRUSY & LIVELY
MILD

VIENNESE BLEND
WIEN 2001 STARBUCKS COFFEE
BALANCED & SWEET
SMOOTH

YUKON BLEND®
STARBUCKS COFFEE
MELLOW & WELL-ROUNDED
SMOOTH

STARBUCKS COFFEE
ZIMBABWE
BALANCED & COMPLEX
SMOOTH

exact specification, and grinding, brewing and serving them to high standards. Every detail matters, including the quality of the water and the time it takes (between 18 and 23 seconds) to make the perfect espresso. This all makes a narrative in itself that provides an element of romance because it goes way beyond measuring a spoonful into a cup and pouring on boiling water. In other words, it's easy to make a bad cup of coffee, but there's something of an art in making a good one.

But the concept of romance then goes beyond this to *romancing the customer*, because Starbucks' people are essential to projecting the brand. The interaction between partner and customer is fundamental. As Howard Behar put it: "We're in the people business serving coffee." So Starbucks needs to hire people who can interact comfortably, be easy, friendly and welcoming, maintain good eye contact, and listen to customers' needs. Natural instinct can be reinforced through training, not only in the ways of coffee but in the values of the brand, starting with respect and dignity. All this helps to retain baristas, who stay longer and get better at their jobs, establishing relationships with regular customers.

Finally, it's about *romancing the senses*, creating the complete experience in store by using all the senses. "The stores are our billboards," therefore they have to express what the brand is all about: the smell of the coffee, the taste, the feel of the furniture, the look of the murals, the sound of the music. If you are to create the right experience, everything matters. Behind every decision is a judgement about truth to the brand: will this support or undermine it?

If these were building blocks added to those already in place, the structure was now becoming stronger. They represented layer upon layer of extra meaning rather than, as is the case with many big brands, a synthesis of meaning on one sheet of paper or in a single diagram. Unilever, for example, uses a "brand key" for all its brands, and this imposes a discipline of concise expression on all its brand managers. Starbucks goes a different route: because it insists on the continuing importance of intuition, it doesn't want to distil its brand into a one-page statement. With Starbucks there is always more, a deeper level of understanding below the one you have achieved, and this makes for a deep and continually evolving brand that still manages to achieve a remarkable degree of consistency.

These were live issues when plans were being made for international development. What is the essence of the Starbucks brand? Can we bottle it and send it over to Japan, and throughout Asia? It turned out that Japan was the first and biggest test for the portability of the brand. It was clear when I talked to Howard Schultz eight years later that the entry to the Japanese market remained vivid. The company took it very seriously, even commissioning a blue-chip consultancy to advise on Japan. For Starbucks, with its leaning towards do-it-yourself, this was almost a revolutionary act. Yet its reaction to the consultancy's recommendations showed Starbucks remaining true to its habitual trust in instinct.

When the study landed, heavily, on the boardroom table, it came out with a clear recommendation not to enter Japan.

There were three main objections:

> **1** Up to 90 percent of the business is take-away, and Japanese consumers would never be comfortable drinking coffee in the street.

> **2** The no-smoking policy would disenfranchise young Japanese, who would avoid stores that banned smoking.

> **3** The high cost of real estate in Japan would necessitate only small stores.

Starbucks listened and discussed the findings. Apart from Canada, it had no experience of overseas operations. Here, at the first time of exploration, they were being heavily warned off by a large, experienced and expensive management consultancy.

Starbucks had been doing its own homework. It had decided that it was interested in the Pacific Rim initially because Europe was already a mature coffee-drinking region. Japan, on the other hand, was a potentially large and developing coffee market. Other companies were starting to develop the market; if Starbucks hesitated, it might find it impossible to enter Japan later. Starbucks' management resources were stretched thin, so it could not afford to hedge its bets by, say, testing Japan at the same time as a "friendly" market such as the UK. It was Japan now or never. So a joint venture was set up with the Sazaby company, whose brand and cultural values were felt to be similar. Yuji Tsunoda, a man who had lived in Los Angeles and believed that Starbucks would appeal to the Japanese, became head of Starbucks in Japan.

For Westerners, perhaps particularly for Americans, there is a wariness about the cultural gulf with Japan. Perhaps this is all the greater as it has reached a level of mythologising through opera. Puccini's *Madame Butterfly* and Sondheim's *Pacific Overtures*, at different poles of a century, have placed the cultural divide at the centre of an artistic exploration. But Japan has generally remained as inscrutable to Western eyes as Noh theatre.

The anecdotal and statistical evidence presented to Starbucks showed that the Japanese liked coffee. Indeed there was a growing local chain called Doutur, with 500 coffee shops. Starbucks believed it could offer higher quality and greater range, while appealing beyond the market of the salaryman to younger people and to women. But there were those three big objections, standing like guards at the gates of Japan. How should Starbucks react? The answer, inevitably, was to stick to the principles of the brand. Starbucks decided to press ahead with its decision to open stores in Japan, and it set the pattern for most of its international developments by entering into a joint venture with a locally focused company. Starbucks addressed the objections that the management consultancy had raised, and answered them in its own way. Howard Schultz still declares that he is not a big believer in consumer research; the Japanese experience will have reinforced his belief that it is real customers buying in your stores who provide the only true picture.

Starbucks' reaction to the consultants' third objection – high rents will mean small stores – was to remain true to the idea of the third place. Because customers who live and work in cities like Tokyo have relatively small homes and long commutes, there was an opportunity for larger stores that would be like extensions of the home. The rents would inevitably be high, but there was a belief that the greater density of population would make it pay to have more spacious stores rather than tiny kiosks.

The second objection – no-smoking stores would deter young Japanese – went to a fundamental principle about the relationship between the product and the brand. Starbucks had a no-smoking policy for a particular reason. It was not to make a health statement or take a moral stance. Because Starbucks placed such a high value on the quality of its coffee, it wanted to protect that quality. Coffee beans are highly absorbent: they take in smells from the environment around them. The simple fact is that smoke harms the coffee bean's flavour and aroma. Starbucks' first two stores in Japan had designated smoking and no-smoking areas, but by the opening of the third store the policy had reverted to no smoking in any Starbucks store. (This policy has remained, even in a country like Spain where there is a tradition of heavy smoking. It has become a differentiating factor that sets Starbucks apart from other coffee houses.)

The first of the consultants' objections – the Japanese would not take to drinking take-away coffee – was harder to counter. It had to be a case of "try it and see." In the event, if there was

Hong Kong *(top)* and Athens *(bottom)*

Shanghai

a cultural taboo about drinking coffee on the street, it was shattered in minutes. The Starbucks team were thrilled to see Japanese businessmen, students, mothers with children, women out shopping, all clutching their paper cups of coffee. And were they actually showing off the Starbucks logo for others on the street to see? It looked like it.

Perhaps what Starbucks had not quite anticipated was the Japanese attraction towards brands they see as cool. Sometimes, as with Hello Kitty, this can be puzzling for people from outside Japan. But if you market your brand with the right degree of cool, the Japanese will spread their love for it by word of mouth. And they want to be seen to be associated with it, whether it's wearing the T shirt, carrying the shopping bag or drinking from the coffee cup. They express their individual likings as groups too, so Starbucks became adopted in batches rather than simply one by one.

Things have settled in Japan since that first caffeine rush, but it remains one of Starbucks' most successful markets. The Japanese service culture and commitment to teamwork played well to Starbucks' own beliefs, so despite fears about a cultural clash between nations there was no cultural clash at a working level. Within five years there were 300 Starbucks stores in Japan, the Japanese partners had their own stock option programme, and the company was listed on the Japanese stock exchange. Whereas Starbucks initially and cautiously saw the target audience as young women, experience showed that the appeal was much broader. Japanese fan sites pop up on the internet. In Tokyo, a Starbucks in an upmarket department store is frequented by wealthy women who bring their children with them, although that had always been considered another cultural taboo.

Yet in other ways Starbucks has adapted to fit into the cultural background, with green-tea Frappuccinos and smaller cups to suit local preferences. Size does not matter – perhaps the hardest message for an American company to accept. The message that was easy to understand was that the traffic count (number of people passing through stores) is 33 percent higher in Japan than in the US. It is interesting too that whereas the take-out business represents 75 percent of sales in the US, it is just 25 percent in Japan.

Starbucks knew from a very early stage that Japan was going to succeed. People understood and liked the brand; there was no cultural disconnection. So it pressed ahead internationally while also moving forward on many other fronts. Stores opened in Singapore and Hawaii. Some of the remoter areas of the US – Arizona, Utah, Idaho – became part of the Starbucks map. A deal was struck with the Westin Hotels group. Continuing product development led to the introduction of Starbucks ice cream, which quickly become the number one brand of coffee ice cream in the US. Starbucks was on a roll and seemed unstoppable. That in turn led to a certain amount of resistance, because people always like to feel they have a choice. Scott Bedbury tells a story about meeting local objectors to Starbucks in San Francisco; their criticisms were that Starbucks would lead to the demise of local shops and reduce choice. The criticisms were largely defused by journalists asking how the employment policies of the local shops compared to Starbucks'. Time has shown that in fact greater choice has been created, because the competition has to improve. If the local shops are good, they survive and thrive.

Starbucks has thrived in almost every market it has entered because it has looked after its relationship with its own people. It knows that brands are ways of making easier connections between people. Everything starts with the attachment between the company and its partners. This results in lower levels of staff turnover; indeed, high levels of retention in a notoriously volatile industry. The relationship with local business partners is important too, because in most international situations Starbucks teams up with a local partner. The only market entry that seems not to have worked – Israel – failed because there was a conflict between the standards Starbucks wished to see (the same as everywhere else) and the standards the partner could deliver. Starbucks withdrew because it felt its brand was being compromised.

That was a blip in a relentless and generally smooth stream of openings in different countries. The Philippines were followed by Taiwan, Thailand, New Zealand and Malaysia, populating the Pacific Rim. The same pattern was followed: hire a local public relations company, eschew advertising, select a flagship location, produce local artwork, retain the core products, adapt fringe products to local tastes, and produce everything to high quality with friendly, trained baristas. These have become entrenched principles.

23rd & Jackson, Seattle

There is a deeply held belief that word of mouth is more authentic, honest and effective than advertising for Starbucks. That puts more responsibility on the brand, and particularly its people, to deliver. So Starbucks takes great care when selecting the right business partners for different markets around the world who will understand its standards and take them to heart. When recruiting starts, new partners (managers and also, at least for first stores, baristas) will be brought to Seattle for training and immersion in the practicalities and the principles. Training lasts between 12 and 16 weeks. Standards for quality, cleanliness, service and speed apply internationally, but the personality of the barista is seen everywhere as the essential expression of the Starbucks brand. The aim is to connect with customers, not just hurry them through. But in the US speed is all-important, whereas in Japan meticulousness is what matters, and people are more prepared to wait in line.

Starbucks started to learn these nuances and find ways to introduce flexibility to local markets. Much of this comes down to trust: everyone trusting the brand, and Starbucks trusting its partners. Local autonomy and personal responsibility are vital to the way Starbucks operates. Two-thirds of employees are part-timers, but Starbucks has always made a point of treating its part-time staff with equity (literally in the sense that stock options are offered to part-timers too). Clearly it is likely to be more difficult to establish trust with employees who have a lesser commitment in terms of hours worked. But if they were to show less commitment in their work, it would undermine the brand, so efforts are taken to look after people well whether they are full-time or part-time. At the same time, there is a realisation and a deep belief that adherence to its principles is an important element of the contract with employees: "If we compromised on quality or on our values, we would have a revolt," said Orin Smith.

This starts to sound almost military in its planning and precision, but the reality is inevitably different. Starbucks remains an entrepreneurial company, perhaps especially in international markets. It has learned to go with its intuition, and this has led to some developments that admittedly are opportunistic. Soon after the opening in Japan, Starbucks was approached by "some great people" (Orin Smith's words). The opportunity was to work in partnership with a local company to open Starbucks stores in the Philippines. The market research suggested that the Philippines was a relatively poor country, and the national income levels might not support much of a Starbucks presence. However, there was a good rapport with the potential partners, so a deal was struck and Starbucks opened in the Philippines in 1997. Beyond all expectations, its presence has grown to more than 50 stores in six years.

I interviewed Orin Smith with two French journalists from *Figaro* and *Le Monde*. The journalists kept returning to the question of prices. "What is the price of a Starbucks coffee in Indonesia? What is the average weekly wage?" Knowing that the two answers are far closer than in the US, they kept professing surprise. If Starbucks were simply a product, their surprise would be understandable, but its success in the Philippines represents clear proof that it is in fact a true brand. People are willing to pay a relatively high price for what they perceive as a treat, a just-affordable luxury, because they are buying much more than simply a cup of coffee.

Asia was well on the way to being Starbucks adopters. Europe beckoned. You sense that there was a slight holding of breath at the prospect. Howard Schultz, in particular, had always regarded Europe and its coffee house tradition in some awe. It seemed that little education would be needed: Europeans understood coffee more deeply than people in other parts of the world. But that made the whole thing all the more challenging. The UK, however, seemed the natural place to start. There were no language difficulties if we discount George Bernard Shaw's dictum about two countries divided by a common language. And there was a chain called the Seattle Coffee Company, with 65 retail locations, that Starbucks could acquire.

The Seattle Coffee Company, as you might imagine from its name, had been built on the Starbucks model by people who had Starbucks connections. It was a benign acquisition: the two companies had a lot in common, including a shared interest in books and literacy. The Seattle Coffee Company was one of the coffee companies that had opened outlets within Waterstone's, the UK's leading bookseller. In the US, Starbucks had had stores within Barnes & Noble bookshops since 1993. The association seemed right to enter into the traditional spirit of European coffee houses as places for ideas and intellectual stimulation. The acquisition went ahead in 1998 and the Seattle Coffee Company stores were quickly rebranded as Starbucks. Overnight, as it appeared to British observers, Starbucks had established itself in the UK.

It took time for this to work financially. Orin Smith smiles ruefully at the cost of British high street rents. Some mistakes were made with locations; some of these mistakes were inherited. Although business was good in terms of people in the coffee houses, it took some time to work towards profitability. Since 2002 this has started to happen, as Starbucks has settled into the market and begun to feel the strength of its brand principles. In particular, the community aspect of the brand (about which I will say more in the next chapter) speaks well to British people, who have a strong identification with the places where they live and work – and a natural tendency to be suspicious of outsiders. With the passing of time Starbucks is seen as less of an outsider as word gently spreads of its involvement in local and national good causes. The UK has grown to be Starbucks' third biggest market in the world, behind the US and Japan.

Cathy Heseltine, the marketing director for Starbucks in the UK, is conscious of simultaneously modelling the UK Starbucks on its antecedents and finding a unique voice and style for the local market. The brand is multi-layered, and little is written down by way of rules or definitions. This gives Starbucks in the UK the flexibility to play slightly different tunes around the pillars of the product itself, commitment to social responsibility and the in-store experience. At the same time there is a determination not to mess with things. Respect and dignity are the starting points for the Starbucks working experience in the UK just as in the US. The emphasis lies on recruiting the right people, training them well (in the London equivalent of the Seattle support center) and building retention by encouraging adult relationships with the company and communities. In the spirit of "It's coffee, stupid," there is a constant reminder of the business's starting point – meetings begin with a coffee tasting.

While the coffee is the immutable core of the experience, other products reflect local tastes. Granola bars sell well in the UK but have yet to make the flight across the Atlantic or the Channel. A new variety of Frappuccino – strawberries and cream – was developed initially for Wimbledon tennis fortnight, but has now been extended to a year-round product. Innocent Drinks, one of the youngest and trendiest brands around, was brought in to develop a new range of fruit drinks for UK stores. "Juicy waters" are selling well, and the Innocent brand provides a complementary but not threatening association for Starbucks.

If Starbucks in the UK has been a patient process, putting down ever deeper roots in communities, success came more quickly in other overseas markets. Hong Kong and Korea were immediately profitable, and the Middle East has grown quietly as Starbucks adapted its style to local sensitivities. "Who will be attracted to Starbucks stores?" is always a key question in the developed markets. The demographic profile has been steadily broadening, but the brand appeals to a wide range of people worldwide. In Arabic countries there are special issues, including the separation of the sexes in Saudi Arabia. The way to handle this is partly shown by the discovery that in the Middle East, the "average customer" is a family, so Starbucks stores are divided into men-only and family areas. Each market has a slightly different take on Starbucks; each market adds a local layer to the mix. In South Korea, this extends to trading in the biggest and tallest Starbucks in the world, a building of five storeys.

Perhaps the most surprising place to find a Starbucks was in Beijing. I had gone there as a tourist over the Millennium New Year and was making my way to the Forbidden City when I came across a Starbucks. Stepping inside, smelling the coffee, hearing the music, I encountered the authentic Starbucks experience. It was not a Chinese experience, though. Starbucks has grown especially fast in Shanghai, opening 15 stores within a year, and South China has become a thriving region. The appeal for the local audience is largely to do with its foreignness and association with comfort, luxury and freedom, qualities that the nation was denied for many years. Starbucks stores are now seen as beacons of China's changing social and commercial environment.

By the end of 2000 there were 3,501 Starbucks stores worldwide; by the end of 2001, 4,709; a year later, 5,886. The latest total, at the beginning of 2004, is 7,500. New shops are opening at the rate of three a day. Like an empire, the sun never sets on Starbucks. Size always carries dangers, particularly if growth is seen as greedy, but Starbucks has gained a momentum

2000
3501
2001
4709
2002
5886 stores

that is hard to stop. There are now Starbucks stores in every US state, yet the market is still relatively untouched (Starbucks has only a 7 percent share of "coffee opportunities" in North America as a whole). Starbucks is located in 34 different countries around the world, yet its purchases represent only 1 percent of the world's coffee; Kraft, Nestlé and Procter & Gamble buy much greater proportions at much lower prices. Even so, Starbucks' visible presence is much more apparent than any of these economically more powerful companies.

Although there are no immediate limits to growth, Starbucks depends on its ability to maintain good relationships, particularly with the local communities where it operates and the farming communities where it sources its coffee. Its ability to grow depends on the good will it can keep generating in the widest possible constituency. The conundrum for Starbucks is to grow big worldwide while retaining the soul of a small company based in Seattle.

TIMELINE

1971 **Seattle**

1972

1973

1974

1975

1976

1977

1978

1979

1980

1981

1982

1983

1984

1985

1986

1987	North-western USA, Canada
1988	
1989	
1990	
1991	California
1992	
1993	Washington
1994	
1995	New York, United Airlines
1996	Japan, Singapore
1997	The Philippines
1998	Taiwan, Thailand, New Zealand, Malaysia, UK (England, Wales, Scotland)
1999	China, Kuwait, Korea, Lebanon
2000	Dubai, Qatar, Bahrain, Saudi Arabia, Australia
2001	Switzerland, Austria
2002	Oman, Indonesia, Germany, Spain, Puerto Rico, Mexico, Greece
2003	Turkey, Chile, Peru, Cyprus, Netherlands (European roasting plant)
2004	France, Costa Rica (Agronomy company)

Chapter Seven
Doing well by doing good

I arranged to meet Neil McClelland at a Starbucks near his office in Victoria, London. I've known Neil for many years, in particular through his work as director of the National Literacy Trust. Ten years ago I had led the project to create the identity for this new charity that aimed to improve literacy skills. Today, the identity still looks fresh, and the National Literacy Trust is celebrating its most significant anniversary yet.

I wanted to talk to Neil because I had seen that Starbucks was promoting a "Book Drop" in association with the Trust. We talked for an hour over coffee, and I learned that Starbucks had been supporting the Trust financially for three years, funding one full-time member of staff. The main project involved Starbucks partners working as volunteers with libraries in 16 local authorities throughout the UK to bring mothers, carers and children into early, enjoyable contact with books and storytelling. Other projects, such as the Book Drop (encouraging customers to donate new books to children), had come along later as the partnership developed. Neil was in no doubt that Starbucks had delivered. His only frustration was that no one had heard of the literacy scheme. Starbucks had been adamant that the purpose of the scheme was to help mothers, children and the partners themselves, not to gain publicity.

I had first come across the link with the National Literacy Trust when I had seen the Christmas 2003 table card in Starbucks' Covent Garden store. There were two main messages on its three sides. One side was about Starbucks' Christmas Blend Whole Beans, a special seasonal blend of beans from Kenya and Guatemala. It was written in the language of the wine buff translated to coffee, with the heading "Special Reserve – Harvest 2003." It read like this:

> "Every year, Starbucks invites the world's
> coffee farmers to send us their finest beans
> for our Special Reserve competition.

This year's Starbucks Special Reserve Blend combines two remarkable regions. From Kenya's equatorial highlands, we found a coffee with an intense, citrusy taste, balanced with delightful winey notes. And from Guatemala's Antigua and San Marcos regions, we found coffees with a sparkling acidity and a hint of cocoa in their profiles.…

In addition to the recognition, there is a greater prize that comes with being named a Starbucks Special Reserve coffee – help for the farming communities that produced the winning coffees."

With after-knowledge I recognise the influence of Cecile Hudon, Seattle-based head of coffee education, in those "winey notes." You might critique them as a piece of writing, but what is more interesting is the way they confront what has become the big issue facing Starbucks. Pressured by anti-globalisation protesters, we need to ask: what is Starbucks doing for the Third World farmers it relies on? What has it been doing throughout its existence as a company? And is that enough?

The table card brings before us, when we turn it to read its other two sides, an extension of the debate. Starbucks needs to think of local as well as global communities. I say "needs," but this is an imperative of relatively recent origin. Corporate social responsibility has been a live issue for companies for less than a decade. When British prime minister Edward Heath used the phrase "unacceptable face of capitalism" in the early 1970s, it took the corporate world by surprise; most business people at that time took their ethical responsibilities rather lightly. There was little thought that companies *needed* to do anything at all for local or global communities, except in a very paternalistic sense. Things have moved on, driven on the one hand by campaigners for environmental and social issues and on the other by the development of branding as a discipline.

What makes Starbucks produce a table card like this? It has very little to do with pushing up sales. It is almost entirely to do with Starbucks' awareness that it is a brand and that it has to demonstrate the reality of that brand: its values, its beliefs, its purpose, beyond selling cups of coffee at a profit. So in this context we see the Starbucks Book Drop. The idea is to help a local child to read, and to encourage reading as an essential element in the learning process, by asking customers to donate new books for children. The store has a box where customers can put their donations. The scheme is run is association with the National Literacy Trust, and Starbucks provides funds and volunteers. It is a small initiative, modelled on a bigger scheme called "All books for children" organised by Starbucks in the US. Some 4,000 British children have benefited in the two years that the scheme has run. But this is only one of many initiatives by Starbucks to put something back into the community.

Starbucks does this to show that its brand values mean something to the company; they are not used merely to generate sales in some way. The aim is also to involve Starbucks' own people in tangible projects that enable them to channel their own energies, interests and beliefs into good causes inside and outside working hours. By doing so they become more rounded people, more satisfied employees and more understanding ambassadors for the brand.

We should look again at the mission statement and its six principles. How do you demonstrate these through a working day of making coffee, collecting used crockery and wiping down tables? It is easier to do so if you see yourself as working in a framework that guides your behaviour, and if you are also encouraged to play a deeper role in the community where you work.

This altruistic streak has always been present in the Starbucks brand. When the first shop opened in Seattle in 1971, there was a natural inclination to reach out to the needy in the neighbourhood. But as the years have passed, Starbucks has given more and more official licence to these philanthropic instincts. As understanding of the brand and its meaning has developed, Starbucks has realised its potential to do good not just by giving donations of money, as most corporations would approach it, but by harnessing the energy of its own people. In 2003 this translated into a new message on its US recruitment leaflets: "Create community."

Starbucks' understanding of its potential role and awareness of the need to engage with the deeper emotions of

its workforce to encourage their commitment started with its successful creation as a public company in 1992. For Howard Schultz in particular, this raised questions about rewards, loyalty and sustaining the brand. His instinct, as with the healthcare provision and stock options, was to build the sense of a team and to set working life within a broader picture. So he became determined to focus more of his attention on local communities, and to encourage the partners in stores to channel their energies into good works.

In 1994, a natural event occurred that made the picture much bigger again. News broke that there had been a severe frost in Brazil, destroying much of the coffee crop. Starbucks bought none of its coffee from Brazil; the quality is generally not high enough, and most of it ends up in cans and jars of instant coffee. But the prospect of shortages meant that prices of coffee started to soar, the big coffee manufacturers immediately hiked their prices, and speculation drove commodity prices up. Starbucks already paid a premium for its coffee, but prices now doubled and were heading higher still.

Starbucks decided not to raise its coffee prices early but to protect customers in the hope that prices would stabilise. In the mean time, it would live off its supply of green beans – coffee bought in advance to ensure it had the quality it needed in sufficient quantity. Then Brazil suffered a second frost, causing further decimation to the crops. Coffee prices rose to 330 percent of the level three months earlier. This threw everything into turmoil. A further complication was the fact that Wall Street was now watching Starbucks' every move.

There were financial expectations to be met, and Wall Street was not inclined to philanthropic gestures.

Orin Smith had just been promoted from chief financial officer to president, and he took command. He decided that Starbucks should manage its way through the crisis, as far as possible cutting costs on backroom operations rather than passing on price rises to customers. The company had grown fast, without real planning, so there were savings to be made. People worked hard, under pressure; but the irresistible price rises to customers did not cover replacement costs of buying new coffee at high prices. A decision was made to buy a large quantity, effectively a year's supply, of Colombian coffee beans. The price was high, but it might go higher. A risk was taken. If prices fell, Starbucks would be left with a lot of expensive coffee beans, but it would have to manage its way through without raising prices to customers to recover its position.

Then, soon after, prices started to come down. Everyone stuck by the decision, without recriminations. In the long run, the economy measures strengthened the company, though it would never have chosen to take them without the impetus of the coffee crisis. They ensured that when the next crisis came, Starbucks would be better placed and stronger. The crisis had also highlighted the plight of the coffee grower, and this had a long-lasting effect on the company.

For many years previously, Dave Olsen, who bought the coffee for Starbucks, had seen worrying signs of distress among the farmers and their crops. Much of the world's coffee crop had been sold at below the price of production to the big coffee manufacturers. The farmers had to skimp, and bad farming practices had been introduced. Pruning was neglected; fertilisers were not bought. In many regions the coffee crops were weakening. Dave Olsen saw at first hand the effects on the farmers he knew. He was convinced that it was in Starbucks' best interests to keep paying a premium price to its farmers for high-quality coffee, and to take other steps to protect them from crippling price reductions.

From this time on, Starbucks knew that its fifth principle – "Contribute positively to our communities and our environment" – could not be compromised. It had never merely been paid lip service, but now it became a driving principle for the brand. When it was exposed to the fluctuations of coffee prices, understood what that did to the farmers and at the same time felt the scrutiny of Wall Street, the effect was to temper the steel of the brand. Decisions had to be made, and those decisions drew on the principles of the brand.

Starbucks emerged a better company from the process. It could have saved itself millions by buying cheaper and poorer coffee. It could have abandoned the farmers who were supplying better quality at a higher price. Most of its customers might not even have noticed. But Starbucks would have noticed. Howard Schultz put it like this: "What, then, would keep us coming into work every day? Higher profits, at the cost of poorer quality? The best people would leave. Morale would fall. The mistake would eventually catch up with us. And the chase would be over."

So now Starbucks decided that the principle of putting things back into its communities should go beyond encouragement. It entered the business model. Starbucks was convinced that not only was it right to have a conscience, but it needed to act on it. It started putting more efforts into developing programmes: both local, around its stores, and in the coffee-growing regions with the farmers. It also decided that the benefits of doing these works were principally to do with its own partners and the communities themselves. The activities were never given PR objectives, so there was no extensive communication about them, partly because the overall thrust consisted of thousands of small initiatives rather than a single massive example of corporate benevolence. Because Starbucks wanted and needed to grow – not least now that it had to keep investors and Wall Street happy – it decided that it could succeed in the long term only by truly engaging with the emotions of its own people. So it set out to provide the environment for its partners to follow their own altruistic tendencies, to grow as people and to develop their skills in the process.

Much of this was building on what Starbucks had already been doing. As the executive who had the most contact with the coffee-growing regions, Dave Olsen had been building case studies and arguments for providing them with support. He established links with CARE, a humanitarian organisation fighting global poverty, for which Starbucks has been one of the largest corporate supporters since 1991. The relationship started relatively small but has grown as Starbucks has

Starbucks works directly with coffee growers

grown, with the company contributing over $2 million to CARE's programmes to fight poverty in coffee-growing communities. Projects to improve water systems, education and medical facilities have been funded in Nicaragua, Guatemala and many other countries.

The Brazil frosts (which happened after the relationship with CARE had started) brought home that something more fundamental needed to be done. How could Starbucks tackle some of the basic causes of poverty in the coffee-growing regions? There were massive economic forces at work here; many other companies were shrugging their shoulders and saying "Not our problem." Coffee is the world's second most heavily traded commodity, after petroleum. Its economic power was apparent to the World Bank, which had encouraged many poor nations to move into coffee growing. This led to a world glut that soon started to drive prices down. As the farmers got less and less money, they were forced deeper into poverty. The only hope of salvation for many farmers is to produce the highest quality coffee that can be sold at a premium. Starbucks buys coffee in this premium range.

The large players in the coffee market have concentrated on buying coffee at the lowest prices on the commodity exchanges. A gap has opened between high-quality arabica coffee grown at altitude, and poorer-quality robusta grown on lower slopes. The figures show that 40 percent of the value of the world's coffee is represented by 17 percent of its volume. Starbucks' policy has been to secure long-term contracts with its coffee suppliers, establishing relationships in the mutual interest of the company and the farmers. So it pays prices that are substantially higher than the prevailing price of commodity-grade coffee. It negotiates prices that are independent of the commodity market, helping to provide stability and predictability for both buyer and sellers. The lessons of the Brazil frosts burned deep into the company's psyche. Starbucks realised that it was in its own interest to ensure a sustainable supply of high-quality coffee.

To achieve that sustainable supply, Starbucks has pursued a number of strategies. These include building direct relationships with farms and cooperatives; negotiating long-term contracts; making affordable credit available to farmers; buying fair trade certified coffees, as well as certified organic and conservation coffees; and investing in health and educational projects that benefit the coffee-farming communities. Starbucks has also developed coffee-sourcing guidelines with Conservation International, an organisation whose mission is to conserve the Earth's natural resources and biodiversity. Under this framework, farmers who meet quality, environmental, social and economic criteria are rewarded with financial incentives and "preferred supplier" status. The arrangements are subject to independent audit.

Part of the strategy is to support fair trade, but Starbucks remains adamant that it selects its coffee first and foremost on the basis of quality. So it will not buy fair trade coffee that does not meet its quality standards. The reality is that the fair trade movement shares the same principles as Starbucks, helping to ensure that coffee farmers receive fair prices for their crops, but the fair trade system still accounts for less than 2 percent of the world's coffee farmers. Fair trade is not the only way to ensure fair prices for farmers, but Starbucks supports it as one of its strategies. You can buy fair trade certified coffee in Starbucks in 19 countries, including the major markets of the US, Japan and the UK. Working with Oxfam, Starbucks is aiming to increase the supply of high-quality fair trade certified coffee from the 16,000 farmers who make up a large cooperative in Oaxaca, Mexico. When American activists organised a "National Call-In Day" against Starbucks, Transfair, the only certifier of fair trade products in the US, described the campaign as "particularly misguided and unfair because it ignores the company's many important contributions to coffee farmers through fair trade and other programs."

Starbucks undoubtedly feels picked on by protesters who ignore the facts. When it challenged one group "Why protest against us and not P&G?" the reply was "Because you care." The anti-globalisation protesters hurt Starbucks in a different way from, say, Nike, McDonald's and Coca-Cola. Starbucks felt a real sense of injustice. It cared about the people who were part of its wider family: the coffee farmers and suppliers. It was hard to be attacked as a rapacious exploiter when it had always paid its partners higher than average wages, given them a valuable stake in the company, provided generous levels of health care, and taken the lead in supporting coffee farmers and their communities. Starbucks had put its own people at the centre of its brand in a way that the protesters' other targets had not. And the sympathies of many in Starbucks, coming from liberal, laidback Seattle, were probably close to the protesters' views. When put together with Starbucks' awareness of the European coffee house tradition to provide places for debate and radical thinking, it all raises the rather ironic picture of anti-globalisation protesters gathering in Starbucks stores around the world to plan their next protest.

Without doubt Starbucks felt discouraged by protests and acts of vandalism against its stores. Many, including Howard Schultz, took the attacks personally and felt misunderstood and misrepresented. Starbucks' response has simply been to plough on, continuing to build its support for coffee-farming communities and the neighbourhoods where it locates its stores. Despite all the protests and bad publicity, it remains more committed than ever to good works, though there has been no public relations blitz to publicise them. Howard Schultz put it like this: "We can both do well and do good. We can be extremely profitable and competitive with a highly regarded brand, and also be respected for treating our people well. In the end, it's not only possible to do both, but you can't really do one without the other."

For those who find sheer altruism hard to imagine, there is a compelling business case that all brands should note. We all have a vested interest in sustainability, even if we don't recognise it. Starbucks does. Early in 2004 it announced that it was establishing the Starbucks Coffee Agronomy Company in Costa Rica. The new venture will have a team of agronomists, quality specialists and sustainability experts to ensure the future availability of high-quality sustainable coffee from Central America. It forms part of Starbucks' effort to get beyond the exporter direct to the farmer, and was prompted by concern that farming practices and husbandry have been critically damaged by years of low prices. Starbucks is acting out of self-interest: it fears that in a few years' time there might not be enough quality coffee available to sustain its projected growth rate. But self-interest and other people's interest can coincide.

Indeed, this is the notion behind Starbucks' practice of encouraging its partners to work in their local communities to support not-for-profit organisations. If you understand this principle, you will understand much of the success of the brand. Satisfaction ratings among staff have placed Starbucks consistently in the top 10 percent of US employers. Material issues – pay and benefits – will account for much of this, but the efforts to encourage volunteering also count. People enjoy working with a company that they perceive as having a soul.

So Starbucks regards support for local communities as an investment: part of its business strategy rather than a series of charitable donations. But even at that level, the charitable donations add up to a major contribution. The way they are organised is characteristic: instead of having the board decide which charities to support each year, Starbucks gets its partners to nominate their favourite causes. The partners give their time and money, and the company supports them with money, materials and encouragement. In the US, two umbrella schemes support volunteering and the championing of not-for-profit organisations by partners. The first, "Make your Mark," matches a $10 contribution for each volunteer hour worked by a partner (or by the partner's family and friends) for a cause of their choice up to a maximum of $1,000. In 2002, 68,000 hours of volunteer time were matched by a $433,000 Starbucks donation. The second scheme, "Choose to give," matches Starbucks funding to an individual partner's philanthropy. The partner chooses the charity and makes a donation; Starbucks donates the same amount and absorbs all the fees and administrative costs. In two years, donations by partners and by Starbucks have exceeded $1 million.

There are numerous other charitable initiatives, most of which originate at the level of the local store. But there are two particular corporate initiatives that tell us something about the Starbucks brand. The first is Urban Coffee Opportunities, a joint venture between Starbucks and the basketball star Magic Johnson. The aim is to open Starbucks stores in deprived, ethnically diverse neighbourhoods such as Harlem in New York. Most of these neighbourhoods have been neglected by business because of their poverty and social problems. When Starbucks enters the community, it lights a beacon for other retailers. The Starbucks stores provide employment and stimulate other business activities that would otherwise stay away. There were 35 of these stores operating in 10 states in 2003.

The second example of corporate philanthropy is the Starbucks Foundation, established by Howard Schultz in 1997 to provide funds for literacy programmes. The Foundation encourages volunteering, and provided $1.7 million to schemes

Magic Johnson

in 2002. It has given grants of $6 million to 625 not-for-profit literacy causes since it was set up; the UK National Literacy Trust venture described earlier in the chapter was one of its beneficiaries. One of its most striking activities is Jumpstart, which matches volunteer college students with pre-school infants from low-income communities. Together, and with support from Starbucks partners, they build children's early language, literacy and social skills.

Part of this is no doubt fuelled by Howard Schultz's origins in Brooklyn. He experienced first-hand what it means to grow up in a neighbourhood that has been deprived of economic sustenance (and the hope that it brings). Even so, American corporate history is full of people who make good despite the economic disadvantages of their upbringing, yet very few of them feel the same need to give something back to the kinds of neighbourhood from which they came.

The real power of Starbucks' approach is that unlike the paternalistic business benefactors of the past, Starbucks does not simply dish out money and then stand back. It does give money, but it also encourages its partners to be active in bringing about beneficial change in their communities. This creates an energetic network, a dynamic movement that produces effects beyond the reach of purely financial donations. Starbucks realises that, for good to come about, good people need to do good. And by doing so, they will each add depth and richness to the Starbucks brand.

THE STARBUCKS FOUNDATION

Chapter Eight
The next port of call

"And so Starbuck found Ahab with a general chart of the oriental archipelagoes spread before him; and another separate one representing the long eastern coasts of the Japanese islands – Niphon, Matsmai, and Sikoke. With his snow-white new ivory leg braced against the screwed leg of his table, and with a long pruning-hook of a jack-knife in his hand, the wondrous old man, with his back to the gangway door, was wrinkling his brow, and tracing his old courses again."

Herman Melville's words from **Moby-Dick** have the ring of mad adventure about them. Another spirit of adventure has taken the modern Starbucks in different directions around the world, and with a different mission. But there is still something obsessive and all-consuming about Starbucks' quest for new territories for its coffee houses.

Starbucks has come further faster than anyone imagined it might. It now employs more than 80,000 people, but still wants to think of itself as a small company. The truth is that Starbucks has grown from a small fish to the proportions of a whale, with the systems and logistical network of a big company. Yet for a vertically integrated company it has become remarkably successful at maintaining quality at every stage of its process, from bean to barista. Its friendly efficiency means that customers stay loyal, visiting Starbucks 18 times a month on average in North America. The equity of the brand continues to have a life of its own, building reputation and trust and enabling Starbucks to keep developing. Part of the company's strength is that it trusts its own people; the likelihood is that the future big idea will come from the imagination of a barista located in whatever proves to be Starbucks' next port of call. Even more certainly that idea will be based around coffee and coffee drinking. Starbucks loves imagination, but is absolutely focused on its core product as the anchor for everything it does.

With good reason, because the coffee effect has been astonishing. The drinking of real coffee has been democratised by Starbucks. In America, and throughout the world, it has filled the gap between the coffee slob and the coffee snob, and made good-quality coffee widely available on a daily basis. It has become a mass-market brand, leaving its flanks exposed to critics on one side ("Too expensive, too upmarket; I prefer instant") or the other ("The coffee's no good"). Coffee snobs like Frasier Crane, living in Seattle, will look down their noses at Starbucks in an effort to maintain their self-image of refinement and tasteful discrimination. They do this while enjoying, in Café Nervosa, all the benefits of ambience and sociability that have been made possible by Starbucks' development of the coffee-drinking marketplace.

Starbucks has been a success almost everywhere in the world it has traded. Its international sales are expected to overtake its domestic US sales – a harder trick to pull off for a brand based on human experiences across the counter than it would be for brands based more on volumes of mechanical transactions. You feel that if McDonald's could find a way to simplify the transaction and do without people altogether, it would. With Starbucks, the transaction itself is almost incidental.

Some people argue that Starbucks grows by manipulation and exploitation; some dedicate websites to their hatred of Starbucks. There is a body of opinion that says all commercial activity involves an effort of persuasion that is manipulative. But is Starbucks more manipulative than most? One fact that suggests not is its low advertising spend. If Starbucks is getting its message across, it is not doing it through advertising. So it seems that a different phenomenon is at work here.

Starbucks is actually one of the purest examples of a brand that we have. It starts with a commodity product – coffee beans – and invests them with extraordinary added value by creating an experience that transcends the simple act of drinking an unnecessary beverage. And this experience becomes an integral part of the daily lives of millions of people. The experience varies from country to country but remains recognisably Starbucks: the brand shows a high degree of adaptability and a readiness to suit itself to changing ways of living. The wi-fi hotspots that enable customers to use wireless mobile computer technology in stores have made Starbucks a world leader in this area; it has understood the increasingly informal approach people take to doing business without fixed offices.

Through such developments, Starbucks has built its reputation and trust over many years. New product developments such as Frappuccino proved to Starbucks that it had earned that level of trust. From trust comes permission to experiment. That permission is extended as long as Starbucks remains true to its core ideals. Along the way Starbucks stretched the brand beyond its core of coffee, reaching into financial services, for example, with the launch in the US in 2003 of its Duetto card: part credit, part loyalty card. The loyalty element keeps the umbilical cord to the coffee experience and stops the card branching off into unrelated territory.

The question Starbucks is increasingly asking is: does the customer trust us enough for us to act as an editor in their lives? Clearly, coffee is an essential element in customers' lifestyle, but what other aspects of their lives can we possibly serve? One of the interesting examples that is moving up Starbucks' agenda is music. Starbucks has played music in its stores for 20 years, and there seems to be an association between relaxed coffee drinking and a background of music.

Timothy Jones was plucked out of the stores in the early 1990s to pursue his musical interests and create taped compilations of music for the stores. Year by year the operation got more serious and more professional. It started making compilations for different times in the day, and customer reactions showed that there was a strong affinity.

From ever-bigger ranges of music, the stores were given the technology to make their own selections to fit local tastes while keeping a close connection to the brand. Through its emotional resonance, music added another sensory layer to the store experience. Certain kinds of music – particularly chart hits – were seen as distant from the brand. Discovery, or in many cases rediscovery of neglected artists, became an explicit aim.

In 1998 Starbucks went a step further and bought Hear Music, a retailer with six stores in California. David Brewster is now a key figure in this development. Hear Music does not just provide the music to play in stores; indeed, its role is becoming increasingly ambitious. It retains a small number of Hear Music outlets that sell CDs, and is opening a flagship store in Santa Monica, Los Angeles in spring 2004. The store

will test whether there is a bigger opportunity to develop a new retailing concept that combines Hear Music and Starbucks.

Whatever the outcome of that venture, music remains integral to the Starbucks experience, not just for customers to listen to while drinking their coffee but to buy and take home as CDs. US Starbucks stores now have listening posts with headphones to try out the range of music. The CDs sold at Starbucks have a high editorial content in terms of both selection and recommendation, with 50-word descriptions provided for each track. There is also a series of artists' choices: CDs with music chosen by, for example, Sheryl Crow, Ray Charles and the Rolling Stones. The compilations are exclusive to Starbucks and offered through its stores. For a music industry in crisis, Starbucks offers something of a lifeline, selling CDs to customers who have been neglected by the music business's obsession with the youth market and the threat of internet downloads. Building on its understanding of its customers' lifestyle, Starbucks has realised that there is an opportunity to fill a gap while continuing to provide a service that remains focused on the in-store experience. Selling CDs is the "frosting on top".

The network thus created is part of the Starbucks effect. A further community, or series of communities, is built around customers' musical tastes: for 1940s jazz, world music, soul, blues, classical. The effect on the music business has been galvanising, and the major labels cooperate with Starbucks to make their artists' work available. This has both revived interest in neglected musicians and helped to introduce new singers: David Gray, for example, appeared on a Starbucks CD before he started selling in millions. Links with local radio stations then spread the ripples even further. Inevitably, this works best in Seattle, where KMTT – The Mountain station plays soft rock and "unplugged" sessions by touring artists. The resulting *On the Mountain* compilations are produced by Hear Music, with radio promotion sending listeners towards Starbucks stores and a proportion of sales being donated to the Wilderness Society.

I digressed into music because it provides evidence that Starbucks still has the ability to reinvent itself and take fresh risks. But we need to return to coffee because Starbucks always does, while keeping an entrepreneurial eye open for opportunities. It remains confident that there is still plenty of room for growth in the coffee market. "Oh, the places you'll go" is the Dr Seuss–like spirit behind Starbucks. It still enjoys planting its flag in exotic parts of the world, and its spirit of adventure and romance remains strong. At the beginning of 2004 the next port of call is Paris, France. There is excitement about how the French, with their strong opinions about coffee and the Americans, will take to Starbucks. But it needs to be restated that the Starbucks approach is not based on heavy advertising to take market share off competitors. It concentrates on growing the overall market. So while Starbucks has thrived, so too have coffee shops of many kinds, including that indomitable specialist, the owner–manager shop. Expect the same to happen in France.

Little of this market growth is achieved by hard selling. Put aside dramatisations of sales techniques you might have seen in such American plays and films as Arthur Miller's *Death of a salesman*, David Mamet's *Glengarry Glen Ross* and Barry Levinson's *Tin men*. These have mythologised the idea of the American hard sell. To get to that point there needs to be a strong base in reality: hard-sell techniques are used in the US to sign people up to everything from sex aids to religion. Yet Starbucks has never gone that route. You might get the odd offer (and strangely enough an offer does sometimes seem an odd thing to find in Starbucks), but the marketing spirit of the company is more akin to "Education, education, education" than "Sell, sell, sell." So a lot of effort goes into training baristas to know their coffee as wine merchants know their wine. The mission to educate the customer in the ways of the bean persists, and is still in stark contrast to the dominant coffee brands that Starbucks came along to challenge. Maxwell House and Nescafé expect very little coffee knowledge of their customers. Indeed, there is a sense in which ignorance is bliss as far as these brands are concerned. Do Nescafé customers ever wonder where the coffee comes from? Few efforts are made to inform them.

Most coffee is sold in supermarkets, and for many years Starbucks refrained from competing in this arena, knowing that the brand experience is hopelessly diluted there – particularly because a pack in a supermarket does not talk to you. With Starbucks, the brand keeps coming back to its people. But there are passionate people in the roasting and packing departments too, and they knew that most of the company's reluctance to enter supermarkets stemmed from the problem of maintaining quality. Coffee beans and ground coffee could sit on shelves for far too long, way past the short "use by" dates that Starbucks insists on. Taken in the last couple of years, the eventual decision to sell Starbucks coffee in US supermarkets was made possible by improvements in packaging technology brought about by Starbucks working closely with its suppliers and maintaining rigorous standards in its roasting plants.

So the product still remains at the centre of the operation. Yet any product, any brand, is at the mercy of the subjective. "I don't like it" is a valid reaction to any product. Personal taste counts. Starbucks is open to subjective dismissal by many people who do not particularly like coffee, or claim not to like Starbucks coffee. All I can observe is that millions of people worldwide do seem to like the coffee. And for those old enough to remember, it is interesting to recall the time before Starbucks and think about the quality of coffee available on the streets of our towns then. Starbucks has raised the overall standard, whatever your individual reaction to the Starbucks product.

Howard Schultz bought Starbucks because he loved the product but saw that it could become better as a social experience. For a brand to have growing power, it needs to be a social animal; it must have the ability to bring people together. The brand acts like a good party host, thinking of the needs and preferences of the guests and providing a suitable setting and atmosphere, yet allowing individuals to adapt the space to their own use.

So Starbucks, despite saying things like "Aim for the unexpected, the offbeat, the clever," will never take idiosyncrasy too far. There has to remain a solidity that comes from a large dose of the expected, the familiar and the unchallenging. Though it may not want to admit it, that is part of its success. We go into Starbucks because we know. We might try other brands because we don't know and they will allow us to risk a little, discover something, perhaps feel a little uneasy in doing so. In Starbucks, we discover only what it has provided the space for us to discover about ourselves; it does that by facilitation, not stimulation.

The reason for not admitting this is the fear of corporate uniformity. Starbucks wants to feel more offbeat than it really is. Yet in providing the literal and metaphorical comfy chair, it ensures that we keep coming back because we enjoy the experience of not being changed, of being at peace with ourselves. The brand is relaxed about being itself and about you being yourself. It does not send out imperatives to "Be like us or else." It is an affirming brand rather than one that challenges you to become something else. It supports you, not transforms you, giving you confidence in your individuality, whether as customer or partner.

Starbucks naturally puts a lot of effort into trying to make this experience as congenial as possible. This means going beyond what many other brands regard as the tools of brand management: the guidelines governing the elements of the identity (logotype, colours, typefaces and so on). The management of the Starbucks brand is built on the principle that *everything matters*. This stems from a system of beliefs and values that is intended to guide every action that anyone representing the company takes. If there is ever any doubt about a decision to be made, you resolve it by thinking about what the brand guides you towards.

Many in these sceptical if not cynical times may find it questionable to base their judgement on a set of beliefs that they did not come to themselves through a process of their own discovery. The strength of the Starbucks brand has been that it has persuaded a large number of people – particularly its own staff and its loyal customers – that its beliefs and values could actually be their own. But this is what happens in any business with a strong awareness of its brand: employees have a formal contract and an informal contract. The informal contract revolves around upholding the brand's values in return for a greater degree of personal expression and involvement at work. For a brand to be effective, it needs to make emotional connections to employees and, through them, to customers – and to respect the physical and emotional needs of both groups. This raises both the expectations and the stakes, leaving brands vulnerable to relatively small slips. Trust built up over years can be lost in a moment. Starbucks has been able to ride out a lot of negative publicity because its foundations have been strong. But it has also been lucky because it has not told its positive story particularly well, not out of arrogance but from a sense of bewildered hurt.

One lesson about brands is inescapable: there is no short cut to success. How many businesses launched in the dot-com boom survived to establish themselves as brands? Very few. How many believed they could offer themselves as brands overnight? Very many. Branding is not like instant coffee; you cannot take a spoonful to get a quick result. It takes time to build a brand because you have to give it strong foundations. The foundations start with a powerful, enduring idea that is embodied in the positive values of the brand. The idea gains resonance, depth and meaning through all the individual and collective actions taken over time. Wrong decisions and false steps can set a brand back, perhaps fatally.

Each individual has a role to play in helping to build the strength of the brand, because everyone affects the way it is perceived. Building a brand is not easy, but if you manage to do it, you create something that is incredibly valuable because people want to be associated with it – perhaps even to be defined by it. That brings a commercial value greater than any amount of marketing or advertising campaigns can create. Unknown 15 years ago, Starbucks is now ranked at number 70 in Interbrand's table of the world's most valuable brands. That is why Howard Schultz says: "The equity of the Starbucks brand is a priceless asset. Every decision we make has to contribute to its sustainability and differentiation."

Above all it is the barista who represents the Starbucks brand. The baristas, particularly in Seattle outside rush hours, are models of non-cloying friendliness. In the store on 1st and Marion when I visit in November 2003, the certificate on the wall says Yumi is partner of the quarter. You can tell why. Within a minute of walking in I receive a glowing smile and an espresso, and we exchange views on the Seattle Art Museum and London.

Particularly in America, but also throughout the world, there is a crisis of trust in the corporate world. The reasons are perfectly understandable. Corporate America has behaved badly, with scandals at Enron, Worldcom and the mutual funds adding to a widespread concern about the power of big business to act against the interests of the individual and the whole planet. The questions customers now ask of companies go way beyond their "value proposition": the right product at the right price. This most basic transaction between brand and customer is soon disposed of. Customers want to know what a brand is going to give the world in return for the cash they hand over for a product. People's faith in governments and institutions is dwindling, so consumers tend more and more to put their faith in brands. But faith – quite rightly – is not easily given, and people feel they have a right to some kind of say in the running of the brand.

This afflicts American brands particularly because much of the world is deeply suspicious of Brand USA in its current expression. American foreign policy fuels anti-Americanism, and naturally American brands suffer. Brand USA is powerful but vulnerable in many parts of the world, including those it might consider its best friends. But the more we get to know the brand through individual representatives and sub-brands, the less vulnerable it becomes.

The brand reasserts its human values to win hearts and minds, rather than relying on its sheer might.

Visiting Seattle makes this a little clearer. The American brand has culturally resonant sub-brands, and Starbucks is a product of one of them. The Seattle sub-brand has been one of the great but relatively unnoticed phenomena of the last thirty years. In 1971 Jimi Hendrix, one of Seattle's most famous sons and exiles, had just died, and Seattle's biggest employer, Boeing, had cut half its staff. Since then, the region has given rise to Starbucks, Amazon and Nike. They represent a different America from Texas, New York or California; not necessarily a kinder, gentler America, but a more globally aware, customer-focused America, a less abrasive but even more optimistic one.

Starbucks is a brand that attempts to do practical good while providing a coffee experience that lightens people's everyday lives. That is an unusual combination, but Starbucks has established a unique place for itself. Its focus on the quality of its coffee remains intense, and gives it the right, the freedom and the power to create communities around its stores. I can think of no other commercial brand that has such ability to be a good neighbour and to make other people good neighbours. The benevolent aspect of the brand is unusual: an antidote to the prevailing public cynicism on the one hand and corporate misbehaviour on the other hand. If it can maintain its ability to encourage good works while providing a good cup of coffee, it could become one of the most powerful and hopeful beacons in the world.

SIX IMPORTANT THINGS FOR OTHER BRANDS TO LEARN FROM THE STARBUCKS STORY

1. Start with your own people: they are the real link to consumers. Exceed the expectations of your people and you will automatically exceed those of your customers.

2. Have strong values that you stick to and know yourself by. Then take decisions according to these values.

3. Ensure there is no gap between your brand values and your actions. Change your actions to fit your values, not the other way round.

4. Keep things fresh by reinventing, but never tamper with the core of what you do.

5. Reach out to communities, making emotional connections between the people who work for you and the places where they work.

6. Remember that every detail matters.

GUINNESS IS GUINNESS ...
THE COLOURFUL STORY OF
A BLACK AND WHITE BRAND
MARK GRIFFITHS

People say "Guinness is Guinness", but it's not as black and white as that. When you pick up that monochrome pint, you're about to taste 250 colourful years of global heritage whose ingredients are astounding innovation, obsessive quality, memorable advertising and a passionate devotion to remaining the world's top stout.

Guinness is Guinness ... tells the story of a truly global brand that's more than just a beer. Today, Guinness is accepted everywhere it trades because it employs local people, uses local resources, adapts to local tastes, advertises with local relevance and reverence *as well as* giving people a product they can enjoy and relax with. All are factors that combine to give a modern meaning to the 75-year old gone-but-not-forgotten advertising slogan, "Guinness is good for you." Does it really taste better in Ireland, its spiritual home? For those who want to get to the bottom of the glass, this book of stories reveals the answer to this and provides fascinating insights into a brand that has inspired warmth in drinkers and non-drinkers alike for a quarter of a millennium.

> "Whether writing about beer or bubble bath, Mark will get under the skin of a brand in order to expose the truth. He'll make you smile one minute and be in your face the next. Writing like that gets my vote every time."
>
> **DAME ANITA RODDICK, FOUNDER, THE BODY SHOP**

If you're interested in Guinness; if you want to learn lessons from one great brand to shine a light on another; if you want to read a good story . . . read on.

BRAND IT LIKE BECKHAM
CREATING A BRAND WITH BALLS
ANDY MILLIGAN

There is no one quite like David Beckham: brilliant footballer, dedicated athlete, fashion model, global icon and all-round celebrity, not to mention husband and father. But Beckham the brand? Well, yes. This book shows David Beckham in a new light: as a man who has harnessed his skills and his growing fame to market himself in the same professional and disciplined way that a successful company markets its brands.

"Brand it like Beckham is an essential textbook for understanding the business of global celebrity. Andy Milligan uses his expert knowledge of why great brands work to provide an invaluable insight into the Beckham marketing phenomenon."

DAVID MAY,
HEAD OF STRATEGIC COMMUNICATIONS, BBC

Here is the story of a new breed of sportsman: one who is as comfortable with the trappings of marketing, fashion and the media as he is with team strips, playing surfaces and training grounds. By looking at the key choices David Beckham has made off the pitch, this book helps us understand how he has achieved his phenomenal commercial success. It provides fresh insights for readers who know about branding, a glimpse of a different side of Beckham for people who know about football, and an inspiring account of individual effort and achievement for all of us.

Brand it like Beckham analyses David Beckham as a brand. No one has looked in detail at Beckham the brand before. This book provides insights for fans of David Beckham, but also for anyone interested in the way that brands really work.